13-6

SOUTH AMERICA
Problems and Prospects

Edited by Irwin Isenberg
United Nations Development Program

THE REFERENCE SHELF
Volume 47   Number 2

THE H. W. WILSON COMPANY   •   New York   •   1975

THE REFERENCE SHELF

The books in this series contain reprints of articles, excerpts from books, and addresses on current issues and social trends in the United States and other countries. There are six separately bound numbers in each volume, all of which are generally published in the same calendar year. One number is a collection of recent speeches; each of the others is devoted to a single subject and gives background information and discussion from various points of view, concluding with a comprehensive bibliography. Books in the series may be purchased individually or on subscription.

Library of Congress Cataloging in Publication Data
Main entry under title:

South America : problems and prospects.

(The Reference shelf ; v. 47, no. 2)
Bibliography: p.
1. South America--Addresses, essays, lectures.
2. South America--Foreign relations--United States.
3. United States--Foreign relations--South America.
I. Isenberg, Irwin. II. Series.
F2208.S68   320.9'8'003   75-12501
ISBN 0-8242-0570-7

PREFACE

South America, it is sometimes said, comes to our attention only when a particularly violent anti-US outburst flares or when one of the region's countries has a spectacular revolution. While this generalization is not entirely accurate, it is true that South America as a whole usually is not an area of major concern even to the student of international affairs. This lack of interest may in part explain why, to this day, the US and South America have not been able to work out a really satisfactory relationship despite decades of discussion at the governmental level, pronouncements of grandiose cooperative plans, and issuance of joint diplomatic communiqués by the hundreds.

Many South American scholars and leaders have viewed the US as an overbearing economic and military colossus insensitive to the feelings of proud peoples, indifferent to the economic needs of the majority, and more interested in stable governments, even if they happen to be repressive, than in governments responsive to popular will. In this view, South America has historically been the object of benign (many would say not so benign) and uninformed neglect from Washington. Even when South America has received unexpected attention, as during the Kennedy Administration, which proclaimed the Alliance for Progress to stimulate economic development, this special concern has been regarded as heavy-handed and patronizing.

From the view of Washington, with its global concerns, South America never has been an area of primary importance. Rather, South America traditionally has been looked upon as a region which supplies the US with numerous important commodities, such as oil, copper, and coffee, and in which US business has massive and profitable investments. Thus, many believe the US has sought to pursue policies which would safeguard the flow of essential materials and protect investments. This may be an entirely reasonable stance in terms of national interest, but it often has led to conflict with what South Americans perceive as their own long-term interests. In any event, US–South American relations have rarely been smooth.

The issues behind this uneasy relationship are complicated because, although the term South America suggests a single unit, the area is one of great diversity. It is composed of eleven countries—Argentina, Bolivia, Brazil, Chile, Colombia, Ecuador, Guyana, Paraguay, Peru, Uruguay, and Venezuela—and several territories. In all, South America has some 220 million people. The area of Brazil alone is greater than that of the continental USA.

Spanish is the official language in all countries except Brazil, where Portuguese is spoken, and Guyana, where English is spoken. This reflects the fact that it was chiefly Spain and Portugal which conquered the local Indian population and colonized South America. In some countries, a large percentage of the people are descended from European immigrants. In other countries, many people are of mixed European and Indian ancestry, while large areas are populated entirely by Indians.

Economically, South America is generally classified as a developing region. Tens of millions of people live in dismal poverty at a subsistence level, suffer from malnutrition and disease, and have little or no access to educational, medical, or other basic services. Yet South America also has a large and prosperous middle class as well as a wealthy and powerful upper class. It has numerous cities such as Rio de Janeiro in Brazil, Buenos Aires in Argentina, and Caracas in Venezuela which are modern, booming, and cosmopolitan. Brazil has been proclaimed as a possible future superpower because of its vast resources, most of which are still untapped. Chile and Venezuela are rich in mineral and oil wealth. Argentina's farmlands are among the most productive in the world. Thus, there is no lack of potential for progress.

Politically, South America has a tangled and confusing history. Despite generations of effort and internal strife, democracy has never been able to establish itself firmly there. Several countries have, at present, democratic governments, but most have various kinds of authoritarian rule. In this century, there have been dozens of coups in South America and numerous political assassinations. In the last ten years, guerrilla movements have flourished to challenge the established regimes in several countries. Violence has bred repression and repression has led to new levels of violence.

This volume presents a view of South America as it is today. The first section offers a selection of articles examining a number of broad issues. The current US foreign-policy approach toward South America as a whole is discussed extensively, and past events that have produced today's position are reviewed.

The second section of this volume presents reports on a number of countries. The articles relate to specific political and economic issues in those countries and point up the diversity of the continent.

The third section is devoted to efforts being made to further economic progress in the region. The excerpts focus on multilateral foreign assistance, but it should be noted that bilateral efforts are also considerable. More importantly, the countries of South America are financing large-scale development efforts on their own.

The fourth section is concerned entirely with Chile because of the tumultuous events of the past few years. Chile was the first country in which voters, with a choice of political parties, elected a Marxist government. That government, voted into power in 1970, was overthrown in a bloody revolution in 1973. It has been charged that the United States Government took an active part in the coup. Now Chile is ruled by a repressive military regime; the junta cracked down hard on opposition views and ruled out elections indefinitely.

The editor wishes to thank the authors and publishers who have granted their permission to reprint the articles in this book.

IRWIN ISENBERG

March 1975

CONTENTS

LATIN AMERICA

I. SOUTH AMERICA: A BROAD VIEW

EDITOR'S INTRODUCTION

In 1958, Vice President Richard M. Nixon was stoned and jeered while on an official trip to South America. The hostility directed then at the US shocked and stunned those who had, at that time, little awareness of the frustrations felt by South Americans, particularly students and other articulate groups. A major frustration stemmed from US military and economic support of several brutal dictatorial regimes. The reason for this policy was the belief by Washington that these regimes, however unpalatable, were nevertheless a bulwark against communism and hence preferable to more democratic but weaker governments friendly with local Marxist groups or unduly influenced by the Soviet Union. Whatever the merits of such a belief in that cold war period, it evoked a large measure of bitterness and fury.

In a major policy innovation, President John F. Kennedy announced the formation of an Alliance for Progress. This was to be a decade of cooperative hemispheric action in the 1960s to stimulate and speed economic and social development in Latin America. However, for a variety of complex reasons, the Alliance never really became the vehicle for progress it was intended to be. During the first year of the Nixon Administration, the grand design of the Alliance was quietly shelved and replaced by more modest programs. Secretary of State Henry A. Kissinger is now trying to move hemispheric relations to a new plane by stressing the need for meaningful collaboration and joint action on economic and political problems.

The first article in this section traces the historic factors that have tended to impede progress. Some traditional features of South American life, however—dominance by the military, the authority of the Catholic Church, the influence of the economic elite—in conjunction with forces now manifesting themselves, may in fact play a positive role in developing countries.

The second extract examines the Alliance for Progress, weighing its contributions and failures. Whatever the problems encountered, substantial economic progress was nonetheless made in a number of important areas.

The third article discusses the efforts of Secretary of State Kissinger to help shape a new working relationship with the countries of South America. As is pointed out, however, serious political and economic differences have emerged and no convenient solutions are in sight.

The next selection notes the power relationships and issues within South America. Basically, the conflict is between the entrenched elite groups and the increasingly vocal majority demanding effective government action to solve long-standing inequities.

The last article in this section stresses the theme of South American assertiveness, but concentrates on the economic reasons for this mood. As the article suggests, South America intends to follow its own economic interests rather than, as in the past, to respond to US interests. It is yet another sign that the US can no longer afford to take South America for granted.

SOCIAL AND POLITICAL TRENDS [1]

The colonial legacy which Spain passed on to Latin America did not facilitate the development of orderly, democratic processes. By 1800 a number of the important features of Latin American society were firmly established: authoritarianism and a tradition of personalism; the intermingling of secular and ecclesiastical, military and civilian

---

[1] From *Latin American Panorama*, pamphlet by Ronald M. Schneider, professor of government, Columbia University. (Headline Series no 178) Foreign Policy Association. '66. p 10-20. Reprinted by permission. Copyright, 1966 by Foreign Policy Association, Inc. 345 E. 46th St. New York 10017.

authority; and a semifeudal order based upon the dominance of large landholders.

The protracted nature of the struggles for independence was another negative factor that contributed heavily to the development of a tradition of force and violence. Moreover, the wars for independence were largely civil wars. . . . The lack of experience in representative processes and self-government and the absence of any accepted principle of legitimacy made the dominance of strong men (*caudillos*) inevitable. Constitutions modeled if not copied from those of the United States and France ignored political and cultural realities. Conflicts over basic questions of political and governmental organization, such as federalism versus centralism, the separation of church and state, tore countries apart; in some cases efforts to resolve these questions monopolized the political arena for decades. A vicious circle of revolt against oppression and oppression to prevent revolt developed in most countries, while dictatorship alternated with anarchy in many.

Brazil was a notable exception. It had the benefit of a constitutional monarchy as a bridge from absolutism to republican democracy. In that subcontinent independence came peacefully when it was proclaimed by the heir to the Portuguese throne in 1822; subsequently the country was held together, despite divisive trends toward regionalism, by an enlightened and liberal monarch who used his authority and prestige to provide a half century of stability while experience was gained in parliamentary government. The transition from monarchy to republic in 1889 was orderly.

Political Developments: A Bird's-eye View

For the great mass of the population of Latin America, independence changed the pattern of daily life very little. The existing economic and social order survived essentially intact, and in the decades following independence political life was almost exclusively the province of the narrowly restricted upper-class elites. Large landowners, the military and the church quickly consolidated their control, although in some of the more economically developed countries they were soon challenged by business and professional groups, who were generally anticlerical and opposed to militarism. The former led the conservative parties, while the latter established liberal parties. The liberals often had to fight their way to power and were frequently ousted by armed force. In very few countries was the ballot box accepted as the final political arbiter until the end of the first century of independence.

The great depression of the thirties ushered in a new period if only by creating problems with which "liberal" governments could not cope. Economic development and social welfare took precedence over personal liberties and representative democracy as effective political issues. New parties and movements arose to deal with these issues, although the older parties remained very much a part of the scene. Thus, while the traditional conservative and liberal parties still exist in many Latin American republics, in only a few, most notably Colombia, are they the major contenders for political power. Even before World War I, radical and socialist parties emerged to enrich political life in those countries with the most extensive industrialization, urbanization and immigration. In Argentina and Chile, the radicals came to share control of the national government. The interwar period also saw the beginning of a variety of social democratic parties, with the American Popular Revolutionary Alliance (APRA) in Peru as a prototype.

In the postwar period there have been several swings of the political pendulum. The great depression tended to breed dictatorships, but in the immediate postwar years civilian reform governments replaced a number of traditional authoritarian regimes. Disillusion with attempts at quick and often radical solutions to basic socioeconomic problems spurred the way for a wave of more conservative administrations, often run by the military. Beginning with the fall of Argentine dictator Juan D. Perón in 1955, these strong men were toppled and succeeded by representative civilian governments. From thirteen military presidents in March 1955, the number dropped to four by 1959. The years 1962 to 1964 witnessed a new wave of military coups, which engulfed eight countries. Once again Argentina was the bellwether. In his effort to reincorporate the Peronist masses into the nation's political life, President Arturo Frondizi overstepped the boundaries laid down by the armed forces and was ousted. In mid-1962, the Peruvian military seized power when electoral results seemed to be favoring the APRA presidential candidate. . . . In April 1964 the vocally leftist regime of João Goulart in Brazil was swept from power by the armed forces, supported by a majority of state governors. Bolivia's floundering national revolutionary regime, headed by Victor Paz Estenssoro, was toppled in November after more than twelve years in power. In Argentina and Peru democratically elected civilian regimes took office within little more than a year after the military coups; in the other six countries progress toward a return to constitutionality took much longer. . . .

The Role of Violence

Violence remains a significant factor of political life in much of the region. . . . Although such violence has long been viewed as stemming from Hispanic character traits, some students of Latin American politics have come to hold that limited violence may be normal to the system and even necessary to its functioning. Given the various types of advantages accruing to those who control the government, emerging groups cannot count upon gaining power through "normal, democratic" means—that is, the organization of majority support. The history of APRA in Peru—three decades as the electoral choice of the majority without ever being allowed to control the machinery of government in its own right—makes this abundantly clear. In many cases government failure to meet legitimate popular demands leads to alienation from the existing institutions and subsequent acts of violence. At other times the fact that political office offers the best opportunities to acquire an economic power base tempts individuals to risk their lives in a coup.

Despite democratic constitutions, few countries of Latin America have yet achieved fully viable representative political systems. In the absence of fundamental political consensus, the need to curb the most divisive effects of unrestrained competition has led several countries to impose some form of institutional restraint upon political activity. In others, the armed forces have felt called upon to moderate excessively intense political conflict, even intervening to remove the president. Yet these same countries occasionally prove to have developed the broadest effective political participation or the highest degree of responsiveness to popular demands and national needs. Thus, except at the extremes of the spectrum, the use of such black-and-white categories as "democracy" or "dictatorship" to describe Latin American governments is of limited value.

Impact of Modernization

The process of modernization and national integration has generated acute socioeconomic tensions and produced serious strains upon immature political systems. The postwar period has witnessed a revolution in the aspirations of large elements of Latin America's population. Many enjoy new material and social advantages; however, for the masses the widening gap between what they have managed to obtain and the much higher level of living which they have come to see as possible has produced a climate of frustration and alienation. Only a handful of countries have experienced real revolutions which have toppled the old elites and elevated new groups to power. Almost everywhere, however, new groups have sprung up in the political arena, diversifying and expanding the electorate. In many countries urban industrial, commercial and financial groups have largely won political control from the conservative landowners. A rapidly growing urban middle class is gaining in political strength through its capabilities for leadership in political parties, its importance in the burgeoning government bureaucracy and its dominant position in the communications media. Urban labor is becoming an increasingly important factor on the political scene. In many countries, however, labor's significance lies in its susceptibility to political manipulation—by the government, by revolutionary leadership or by moderate reform parties—rather than in its limited capabilities for independent action.

The fundamental social, economic and political changes which are so noticeable in the cities are only beginning to penetrate the vast rural areas. Peasants are largely shut off from an effective role in normal political activities but are increasingly being reached by extremist agitators. The discontent of this awakening group, as well as of the urban masses, has been reflected in a tendency to follow those who offer radical solutions. But it should also be noted that aroused democratic groups are increasingly active in the countryside.

The impact of these developments has been evident, as noted above, in the proliferation of political parties. Modern political parties, with a greater emphasis upon organization at the grass-roots level, are beginning to serve as vehicles through which emerging social groups can make an entrance into the political life of the nation. In recent years, national revolutionary, social democratic and Christian democratic parties have won the support of sizable segments of the electorate. Often working in cooperation with labor organizations, they have caused parties which in the past catered to propertied groups to modify their appeals. The moderate reformers realize that if they fail to satisfy the demands of the lower classes, political power may slip into the hands of extremist leaders. Hence they seek to transform the existing order in a gradual and peaceful manner.

Role of the Church

The Catholic Church in most Latin American countries has sought in recent years to break away from its traditional image as a pillar of the established order and to identify increasingly with the forces of peaceful reform. The church played a significant role in the overthrow of dictatorial regimes in Argentina, Colombia and Venezuela during the 1955-58 period and has become far more active in the social action sphere, although its influence varies widely from country to country. Not all elements of the clergy have participated in the shift to a more liberal position, while some have gone over to the far Left. Generally, however, the influence of the ultraconservatives is waning, while modernizing tendencies enhance the church's capabilities to play a moderating role in areas where it retains vigorous roots.

These changes in the sociopolitical position of the church have contributed to the rise of the Christian Democratic movement, which has demonstrated impressive vitality in recent years. . . .

Landholders and Middle Classes

Although its power has been greatly eroded in recent decades, the traditional large landowning class is still very influential in the political life of most Latin American nations. The large-estate owners retain great social prestige, substantial economic importance and considerable political power, particularly in rural areas. In those countries where industrialization has gone forward, many of the old economic elite have diversified their investments and become important in urban as well as agricultural affairs. Partly as a consequence of this fact, Latin America's industrialists and businessmen do not make up a homogeneous group or follow the same pattern of political alliances from one country to another. Those oriented primarily toward mining or export agriculture may often come into conflict with those involved in the production of consumer goods for an expanding internal market.

With the increased industrialization and modernization of Latin America and the consequent broadening of sources of economic power, these groups may lose much of their political power and influence over government decision making, but in most countries their acquiescence will be a prerequisite for substantial economic reforms for at least another decade. Fortunately, there are in most countries a significant number of younger entrepreneurs who do not see the necessity for change as incompatible with their interests. Unlike the older oligarchs, they often appear willing to accept basic social and political changes, which may entail a decline in their relative power position, so long as their economic well-being and social status are not severely jeopardized.

Professionals and self-employed tradesmen in Latin America may identify themselves either with some segment of the elite or with the growing middle sectors, depending upon the particular circumstances of their society. Some in the middle class frequently look to the upper class for political values and direction, although other elements of this stratum feel closer to urban labor. Thus, in many Latin American countries these middle-class groups can be discussed meaningfully only in relationship to the groups above and below them.

"Militarism" in Latin America

The single most important factor in Latin American political life has been and continues to be the military. Traditionally the values of the military have differed from those of civilians in terms of a far greater emphasis upon honor, glory, order and discipline. Traditionally, too, the military has been associated with the narrow ruling groups, often participating in power struggles between rival factions of these groups. In this role it has contributed little to long-run stability.

But the Latin American military has also played another and more constructive role: that of nation building. . . . Throughout the first century of independence, at a time when regionalism often reigned supreme, military service helped to nationalize, socialize and politicize sizable segments of the population.

Beyond this, the military has spread literacy, public health and basic technical training. Its contribution to economic development has been substantial: more than any other group it helped to create modern transportation and communications networks. It played a major part in opening up the interior of South America, notably in Brazil, Bolivia and Peru. Thus, long before the term was coined in this country, the Latin American military was deeply involved in "civic action programs."

To be sure, civic action programs . . . have had ambivalent effects upon the political activities of the military in various countries of the area. For while they are intended to divert military energies to constructive aspects of nation building and to improve relations between the armed forces and civilian populations, the programs inevitably extend the involvement of the military in areas of government previously left to civilian authorities.

Yet to say, as has so often been said, that the dominant role of the military in Latin America has been *the* primary obstacle to the development of political democracy leads too frequently to a confusion of cause and symptom. Often it was the failure of civilian democratic governments which brought the military into politics, or back into politics or more deeply into politics. Civilians who one day decried military intervention in the affairs of goverment the next day pleaded with the military to intervene. Established elites often sought the help of the armed forces in curbing leftist experiments, while emerging classes looked for military allies in efforts to topple the older order.

In recent years, it should be noted, the role of the military has been changing as the outlook of the armed forces has become more modern. Where this has occurred, the military has contributed constructively to national integration and economic development, while at the same time defending the basic institutions of society. Moreover, army leadership tends increasingly to be drawn from middle-class sectors, and even from the working and peasant classes, and to represent national rather than elite-class interests. And more and more the military finds that it has to compete with new emerging groups for influence over national policy. In some cases it has reacted to this challenge by seizing power and restricting mass-based political parties.

WAS THE ALLIANCE FOR PROGRESS A FAILURE? [2]

Latin America is clearly assuming command of its own destinies. But the basic causes of this change have yet to be established. Until further research isolates and documents them, Eduardo Frei Montalva, former president of Chile, writing in *Foreign Affairs* in October 1971, offers an illuminating interpretation of some of the dynamic forces shaping contemporary Latin American history.

To Dr. Frei, "the present juncture is a second revolution, a long-delayed sequel to the first and great one—the Wars of Independence of 1810-1830—an attempt . . . by Latin America . . . to create a way of life for its peoples that they could truly call their own." The primary force in this second revolution is a popular nationalism, the content of which—precisely because it is a people's nationalism and no longer one of upper-class privilege—is an array of values and concepts of social reconstruction to incorporate the "formerly disenfranchised majorities into the political, economic, social and cultural stream" of Latin American society. . . .

When students of Latin America begin to analyze the

[2] From *Latin America: Toward a New Nationalism*, pamphlet by Ben S. Stephansky, former US ambassador to Bolivia and to the Organization of American States. (Headline Series no 211) Foreign Policy Association. '72. p 19, 21-30. Reprinted by permission. Copyright, 1972 by Foreign Policy Association, Inc. 345 E. 46th St. New York 10017.

factors which launched the region's second revolution, they will no doubt find that one of the favorable conditions was a growing confidence among a majority of the countries in their development capabilities and potentials. There were two reasons for this:

The first was the "discovery," as experience accumulated during the first United Nations Development Decade in the 1960s, that among the three large areas of the less-developed world (Africa, most of Asia and Latin America), Latin America's development level set it apart. Latin America is the Western world's least modernized region, into whose dynamic growth system it has been imperfectly incorporated. Yet, Latin America has reached a development threshold which most of Asia and Africa will probably not achieve for perhaps another generation. The average per capita income of Latin America is more than three times that of the less-developed nations of Asia and Africa. The per capita gross national product (GNP) of half a dozen of the larger Latin American countries is very near the level reached by a number of advanced countries after World War II, such as Japan, Italy, Austria, the Netherlands and Finland. Latin America is also well ahead of most of Asia and Africa in its level of industrialization, over 25 percent of the GNP for the region originating from industry. By this measure as well, Latin America has reached a stage of development comparable to that of some advanced countries after World War II. To be sure, the region still faces formidable problems in transforming economic and social institutions that lack sufficient dynamism to satisfy the needs and demands of a rapidly growing population; nonetheless, in the 1960s its rates of economic growth were impressive when measured against comparable periods in Europe and North America.

The second was the Alliance for Progress. Much has been written and said about its frustrations and failures. . . .

Alliance Shortcomings

The now-standard indictment of the Alliance for Progress . . . lists the following shortcomings: (1) The Alliance goals were overambitious and therefore inevitably invited frustration and disappointment. (2) Because of US leadership in its formulation, the charter of Punta del Este, the Alliance's basic document drawn up in the summer of 1961, took on the character of a US master plan for Latin America, and therefore encountered strong resistance in that area. The failure to reach its goals also unduly identified the US with both the failure and the ensuing frustrations. (3) The political objective of the charter—economic development within a framework of democratic government—was both unrealistic and "interventionist"; it, too, therefore was doomed to fail. (4) The cold war context of the Alliance, its unstated but understood objective of preventing further "Cuba-type" Communist footholds in Latin America, tempted the United States to rely inordinately upon "internal security" programs of military, police and "counter-insurgency" training. These programs inhibited legitimate movements for social change, threw the weight of US support to status quo and military regimes, and alienated popular and student groups and the intellectual community from the Alliance. (5) When the cold war began to lose its urgency . . . [other problems took priority in the US]. (6) The Alliance was too often utilized to impose pressure on behalf of US private investment interests. . . . (7) Finally, sales of expensive military equipment to Latin American countries evoked increasing criticism in the US. Congress reacted by amending the Foreign Assistance Act so as to reduce economic assistance funds by the amounts spent for "sophisticated" military equipment by any government . . . or to terminate assistance entirely to a country spending an unnecessarily large percentage of its development resources on such purchases. . . . In turn, Latin American countries, under the pressures of their military establishments, rejected these restrictions angrily as unwarranted incursions of the Alliance in domestic defense decisions.

Many of these criticisms of the Alliance are valid, particularly the ones pointed at the subordination of development objectives, social and economic, to US "strategic" objectives, the meddlesome interventions in Latin America's internal life and the efforts to employ aid to obtain advantages for private investors. . . .

It is small comfort to learn that the US, in its relations with the Alliance, succumbed to the self-serving habits of all the powerful nations in their donor roles—a shortcoming equally discernible in "capitalist" and "socialist" countries. Herein originates the strongest argument for multilaterally as against bilaterally administered development assistance— although the multilateral agencies are not immune either to pressures from the larger donor nations. But, while the Alliance can be indicted for its "arrogance of power," there was another side to the Alliance, a more hopeful side, that contributed significantly to Latin America's confidence in its development capabilities and that may, in longer perspective, soften some of the sharper injustices Latin America endured in the Alliance years.

Some Alliance Achievements

One can take issue with the critical view that Alliance objectives were too ambitious, that they offered, in the words of critics, "instant development," too sweeping in scope and in too short a time. It is true that the Alliance failed to achieve many of the development targets. . . . But it was not so much the levels of the targets as it was the elementary "state of the development arts" that was the cause of the apparent failure. It is easy to forget that both the theory and the practice of the development arts were still quite new in 1960. The Marshall Plan [US aid to Western Europe after World War II], Point Four [an early name for US technical assistance to the developing countries] and, during its first decade, the World Bank policy of funding mainly "bankable" major infrastructure or large capital projects (like road building in Colombia and the Volta Redonda steel plant in Brazil) offered little reliable experience for the less-developed world; and Latin America, along with other developing regions, was destined to go through the painful experience during the 1960s of learning that development was a difficult and lengthy process. Yet, it is noteworthy that, after a decade's experience in Latin America under the Alliance, the authoritative verdict regarding the charter's targets is not that they were too ambitious but rather that they were probably too modest. . . .

Perhaps the measure of the excessive modesty of the Alliance development targets is the degree to which significant progress was made in most of the target areas even though the target levels may not have been reached. The OAS [Organization of American States] Secretariat's analysis of the ten-year period records some very impressive achievements. It compares the progress of the 1960s with that of the 1950s as a more realistic evaluation of the Alliance, rather than judging the Alliance by its own imperfectly projected goals. By this historical standard, the OAS Secretariat lists the following areas of progress:

1. Compared to the "situation in the 1950s, when the growth rate . . . was declining and the external sector was checked, growth was successfully stepped up throughout the 1960s, especially during the second half of that decade . . . very close to the 2.5 percent per capita set forth in the charter of Punta del Este . . . and this rate was surpassed in seven . . . countries." . . .

2. "The annual growth rate of the industrial sector was 6.2 percent during the decade [of the 1960s] . . ." surpassing the rate of the previous decade.

3. "The substantial progress achieved in primary education, reduction of illiteracy, and expansion of secondary and higher education will make it possible to achieve increases

in labor productivity and faster dissemination of technological progress."

4. "Expansion of health benefits and greater benefits and
greater government activity in housing contributed to an
improvement in environmental conditions . . . progress in
educational, sanitary and environmental services . . . is very
significant and has the potential of offsetting possible regres-
sive trends in income distribution."

5. "Unlike the situation in the previous decade, export
expansion was of major importance as a dynamic growth
factor, and it was accompanied by a diversification in markets and in products exported. . . . These favorable developments . . . were reflected during the second half of the
decade in an appreciable increase in import capacity . . .
[and] in [an improved] balance-of-payments position that
serves as a better basis for future growth. . . ."

6. While there was "limited progress in Latin American
economic integration," there was "a significant increase"
in "transportation infrastructure . . . [and] in the number of
transport projects under way . . . at the end of the decade."

7. There was "substantial progress achieved in tax policies, tax collection and fiscal administration," thus greatly
improving the public sector's role in savings and overall investment.

The OAS Secretariat noted insufficient progress in agriculture, agrarian reform, and science and technology, although somewhat improved over the previous decade. The
perspective of a full decade, however, led the OAS Secretariat to conclude that the Alliance recorded "improvement
in growth, of preparation of bases for further development,
and of institutional progress in the public sector." The
"success" or the "failure" of the Alliance will undoubtedly
continue to be debated; but it appears, as time proceeds,
that its growth-inducing features were far more important
than they appeared to be at the time the Alliance was in
operation.

Enduring Contributions

But the major and enduring contributions of the Alliance transcend the improved growth threshold established for Latin America, important as that was. These contributions were more profoundly understood and appreciated in Latin America than in the US; and they forever separated the region from its previously erratic, aimless and floundering perception of development capabilities and potentials. The most noteworthy include:

1. The emergence and increasing sophistication of systematic economic planning. At the time the Alliance began, planning was in an elementary stage, and only two or three countries had formulated partial development plans. Ten years later, most Latin American countries had devised their development plans and had remarkably increased their capability to establish priorities and to select and design development projects.

2. The growing capability of managing multilateral and domestic development institutions. In the period of a decade, Latin America enormously advanced in its understanding and skill in operating newly established development institutions, nonexistent before the Alliance, such as the Inter-American Development Bank and the Social Progress Trust Fund, just beginning to operate at the inception of the Alliance; . . . about twenty-six domestic development banks and development corporations; and the beginnings, at least, of institutions for regional economic integration. This progress was reflected in an equally impressive increasing ability to deal with the World Bank, the International Monetary Fund, the Export-Import Bank, and with foreign countries seeking new investment and trade relations in Latin America.

3. The implementation of regional economic integration. Although the idea of Latin American economic integration goes back to at least the beginning of the century, the US

28The Reference Shelf

did not alter its largely passive and even negative attitude
toward the concept until the middle years of the Alliance for
Progress. Then in 1967 at a meeting of Latin American
presidents in Punta del Este, the US made a formal commitment to cooperate in Latin America's integration effort.
While the verdict on integration is that it proceeded at a
disappointingly slow pace during the Alliance, very important beginnings were made among subregional groups. . . .

4. The ripening of a continent-wide "development consciousness," connecting economic development to social development. In the words of the OAS Secretariat, "the great
value of the charter of Punta del Este was to represent ac-
ceptance at the hemisphere level of a broad concept of
Latin American economic and social development . . . the
need for economic development to be accompanied by deep
social feeling and . . . institutional change." While this consciousness "is doubtless a basic truth which cannot be measured quantitatively," it has pervaded the politics and social
movements of virtually all the countries of the hemisphere.

5. The sturdier growth of the concept of "self-help"
and self-reliance in development efforts. Partly as a result of
painful experiences with the overweening presence of the
US, but mainly as a result of the rigors of coping with development problems, Latin America learned during the Alliance that development was not an externally bestowed
"miracle," but required sacrifice, discipline and sustained
effort. The evidence is increasingly persuasive that after ten
years of the Alliance, Latin America can discriminate far
more clearly than it could in 1961 between the external assistance it will require in the future and the responsibility
it retains and must exercise for its own development decisions.

6. Finally, the Alliance produced a new "stable" of development talent. This was perhaps the most encouraging
product of the decade—the emergence of young, technically
trained people, schooled in the domestic and multilateral
Alliance institutions, demonstrating that Latin America

possessed the human resources for its own development future.

These are some of the "nonquantifiable" but more durable contributions of the Alliance. If it generated disenchantments, these were outweighed by a decade's variety of experience that strengthened the region's confidence in its ability to manage and shape its own world. This, in the end, was the Alliance's historical mission, and the US, instead of turning away, should welcome Latin America's new independence as the larger evidence of the Alliance's success, in which, however imperfectly, it had a major share.

KISSINGER'S "NEW DIALOGUE" [3]

The sad truth about US–Latin American relations is that ten decades of intercontinental conferences, "new dialogues," and proclamations of friendship have done little to redress the hemispheric imbalance: Latin America remains poor and frustrated; the US remains rich and powerful.

Everything else follows from this. US programs of trade and aid are merely frosting on the cake. The reality is that forty years of "good neighborliness" have not enabled a single Latin American nation to step out of poverty and underdevelopment.

Any "new relationship"—and the possibility is once again being aired—must therefore be based on a realistic appraisal of the basic relationship between the US and Latin America. And if the Latins want to get rich and the Americans want to stay rich, the conclusion may well be that their interests are incompatible. To change the relationship, a clash of interests may therefore be inevitable.

Traditionally, Washington's policy toward the southern continent has consisted of negligent paternalism. And by constantly asking for a "new relationship" and complaining

[3] From article by Alan Riding, specialist in Latin American affairs. *Saturday Review/World*. 1:12-15. Ap. 20, '74. Reprinted by permission.

that "the US doesn't care," Latin America has only encouraged this paternalism. Talking from a position of weakness, Latin America has only obtained reluctant charity; talking from a position of strength, Washington has only responded to threats to its interests.

To smooth over the wrinkles in this traditional relationship, endless numbers of inter-American organizations and committees have been created. Almost monthly, one or the other produces yet another study or resolution or declaration on the state of relations between the regions. . . . There are some diplomats who have spent their working lives going from one of these committees to another. . . .

But once the organizations and the reports are set aside— so repetitive, so depressing, so accurate, yet so irrelevant— Washington's policy toward Latin America can be seen in all its simplicity and nakedness: it involves maintaining the continent generally within Washington's sphere of influence, preventing the emergence of leftist regimes, protecting US investments, developing a market for US exports, and securing the region as a fount of raw materials. Liberalism apart, there is nothing wrong with this. Washington defends its interests as it sees them—and it softens the blow with some charity and rhetoric.

The Alliance for Progress, launched with such flair by President Kennedy in 1961, fell perfectly into this pattern. It was realism wrapped in good will. Once the CIA-guided invasion of Cuba had collapsed on the beaches of the Bay of Pigs [in 1961], Washington accepted the permanence of Fidel Castro and sought to neutralize his influence through the Alliance for Progress. [There are now signs that Washington is willing to deal with the Castro regime in Cuba on a limited basis.—Ed.] Right-wing dictatorships therefore were frowned upon, democracies were bolstered, and economic and social reform was encouraged. This prong of the Alliance was aimed at defusing popular unrest. The other prong—that of sharing the grim secrets of counter-insurgency with Latin America's armies and police forces—

was to prevent this popular unrest from taking political shape.

Throughout the sixties, US advisers therefore helped Latin American governments to fight the extreme Left until the guerrillas of the continent were virtually exterminated. And as the ruling oligarchies modernized themselves to face the new challenges of the masses, Washington found that it could relax its vigil over the continent and concentrate on the problems of Southeast Asia. The Alliance for Progress consequently lost impetus and resources.

But there were occasional problems that required attention. In April 1964 Brazil's left-leaning government of President João Goulart was ousted with Washington's blessing. A few months later the defeat of the Marxist Salvador Allende in Chile's presidential elections was assisted by US funds. In 1965 the Dominican Republic was invaded by US Marines "to prevent another Cuba." And in 1968 a leftist military regime in Peru was boycotted—though it could not be ousted—after it had nationalized a major US oil company. The collapse of the leftist regime of General Juan José Torres in Bolivia in 1971, however, was a relief to Washington. And the successful termination of its campaign against the Allende government in Chile between November 1970 and September 1973 was toasted with champagne in Washington.

But none of these "occasional problems" were sufficient to alter US policy toward the continent. In fact, in October 1969, in his only major speech on Latin America, President Nixon felt so confident about the region that he formally buried the Alliance for Progress and announced the start of a "more mature" relationship based on trade, not aid. Two years later this new maturity meant burdening Latin American products with a 10 percent import surcharge even though the continent had a huge trade deficit with the US. But in November 1971 Mr. Nixon dispatched his special assistant, Robert Finch, around the continent to "confirm" his good will. And in May of last year, the then Secretary

of State William Rogers traveled Latin America to an-
nounce his stillborn "new relationship."

Now, with [Secretary of State] Henry Kissinger (who
was quoted as once having characterized Latin America as
"a dagger pointing at the heart of the Antarctic") in the
State Department, the proclamation of yet another "new
dialogue" is echoing over the bones of the decades-old "special relationship." ...

But Dr. Kissinger is not a man given to political roman-
ticism. This "new dialogue" is therefore different because
it starts from a premise of realism rather than guilt. The
words are the same, but the mood reflects a change in the
basic relationship between the US and Latin America.
Washington has begun shaping a new policy toward Latin
America because suddenly it has an interest to defend. And
Latin America is responding differently to the invitation of
a "new relationship" because suddenly it has acquired relative strength.

The change can be explained in one phrase: the energy
crisis. It is, of course, an oversimplification, but the impact
of the energy crisis on the attitudes and policies of the US
and Latin America threatens to transform the basic relationship between the two regions more than do any number of conferences and declarations.

For many Latin American countries, the hike in world
oil prices has meant serious short-term economic problems,
not least through increased inflationary pressures. But it
has also left another mark. Many governments are now becoming aware that the terms of trade for their raw-material
exports might also be altered dramatically if they follow the
Arab example and join forces to push up world prices.

In a sense, Latin America has been preparing for such
an action for over a decade. The mounting disillusionment
with inter-American and even international forums has
slowly pushed Latin America into the Third World camp
of militancy. Only a few countries of the region are encom-
passed by the political nonaligned nations movement, but

governments with the most divergent ideologies—such as Brazil and Peru—stand together on most world economic issues. In their relations with the US, Latin American governments disagree on such political questions as Cuba, but they face Washington as a bloc on trade, investment, and monetary issues.

From Dr. Kissinger's global perspective, the danger that Third World producers' cartels may spread from oil to other key raw materials is therefore apparent. And if they do spread, the industrialized world will be convulsed even more than now. Latin America thus takes on strategic significance: By wooing the continent, the US not only would divide and weaken the Third World but also would assure itself a continued supply of cheap raw materials.

As with the Alliance for Progress, the first coherent US policy toward Latin America in thirteen years has grown out of necessity and self-interest rather than good will and justice.

Though he is by no means a specialist in Latin American affairs, Dr. Kissinger nevertheless has found a place for the continent in his global pattern of power. And once his Atlantic Community [of joint cooperative action by the industrialized nations] had been rejected by a restive Western Europe, his concept of a Western Hemisphere Community's linking the US and Latin America seemed all the more necessary. Ideally, such a community—a concept of mutual obligations and understanding rather than a juridical body—would bring Latin America closer to Washington and would separate the continent from the Third World.

The community idea was launched in Dr. Kissinger's masterly opening statement to the Mexico City Foreign Ministers' Conference ... [in] February [1974]. ...

He began by stressing the interdependence of world regions today and the need for collaboration and cooperation between "consumers and producers, the affluent and the poor, the free and the oppressed, the mighty and the weak." Then came the acorn. "So let us begin in this hemi-

sphere. . . . The world community which we seek to build
should have a Western Hemisphere Community as one of
its central pillars." Soon "our community" already seemed
to exist. "We must renew our political commitment to a
Western Hemisphere system," he went on. "In this way,
the Western Hemisphere Community can make its voice and
interests felt in the world."

As proof of Washington's good will, he cited the . . .
Agreement of Principles for a new canal treaty signed by
the US and Panama and the . . . agreement on compensation
to expropriated US companies signed with Peru. . . . For the
future, he proposed a mechanism for settling disputes between US companies and Latin American governments without involving Washington, and he suggested an "equitable
interim accord" for resolving the problem of US fishing
boats arrested inside the two-hundred-mile territorial waters
claimed by several Pacific-coast nations.

"But we cannot achieve our goals by remedying specific
grievances," he said. "A special community can emerge only
if we infuse it with life and substance." Wisely, he chose to
be vague on the details, but the concept was clear. Members of the community would assume an obligation to con-
sult at regular intervals and, in effect, to take no unilateral
measures (such as joining raw-material producers' cartels)
to harm the spirit of the community.

The reaction of Latin America was immediately negative. Most large countries prefer to deal bilaterally, rather
than *en bloc*, with Washington. A few minutes before Dr.
Kissinger had spoken, Mexico's President Luis Echeverría
had also declared categorically that "Latin America forms
part of the Third World." Brazil, supposedly Washington's
closest ally on the continent, had already succeeded in
sinking Dr. Kissinger's proposal for an energy debate for
fear of offending the Arab oil producers that supply two
thirds of its oil needs. Venezuela, the continent's major oil
exporter, felt under siege from Washington for its solidarity
with the Arabs and responded by urging the producers of

copper, bauxite, iron ore, manganese, and other key raw materials to follow the example of the Arabs. Argentina, which is currently strengthening its ties with Western Europe, was not interested in the community. Peru's left-leaning military rulers felt that they had little in common with Washington.

Even smaller countries were suspicious. Guyana's ... foreign minister ... asked how a Western Hemisphere Community could exist between one superpower and twenty-four poor nations and without the inclusion of Cuba or Canada.

But as the conference continued, it became clear that Dr. Kissinger had made an offer that Latin America could not refuse. The Latin and Caribbean foreign ministers had wanted to talk frankly and informally about a whole range of issues—aid, trade, and monetary questions, US economic coercion, multinational corporations, transfer of technology, and so on—and Dr. Kissinger was simply saying, "Fine, let's do so in an inter-American spirit." His presumption was that regular consultations and negotiations will create natural reciprocal obligations, even though the word *community* is abandoned. After all, as the secretary told the foreign ministers privately, hegemony comes from power, not words. So in the final Declaration, the foreign ministers "agreed that interdependence has become a physical and moral imperative and that a new vigorous spirit of inter-American solidarity is therefore essential."

Thus Latin America had finally found a place in Kissinger's view of the world. At last, US diplomats and even businessmen scattered around the continent knew that Washington's new policy was aimed at preventing Latin America from joining the Third World as an unseemly threat to the industrialized nations.

... The dialogue continues, and the negotiation toughens. Divisions are apparent in the Latin camp—some governments are prepared to brave on and to fight for a new world economic order; others would prefer to extract short-term advantages from Washington—but the confrontation is more equally balanced than before.

Washington still has huge bargaining power—and Dr. Kissinger insists on bringing congressional leaders for his talks with Latin America to secure his freedom of action—but US concessions will be unavoidable. It could mean an early end to the economic blockade of Cuba or a generous new canal treaty for Panama or specialized preferences for the manufactured exports of the continent. [Discussions on the Panama treaty have already taken place.—Ed.] But the strategy is clear: Washington wants Latin America back in its camp and is prepared to pay to achieve this end.

Economic relations are the obstacle, because political harmony largely exists. With the Allende regime [in Chile] removed from the map of Latin America, Dr. Kissinger could indeed afford to proclaim in Mexico that "we will not impose our political preferences; we will not intervene in the domestic affairs of others." After all, the vast majority of Latin American governments are already to Washington's preference. Generals rule in Brazil, Paraguay, Uruguay, Chile, Bolivia, Peru, Ecuador, Panama, Nicaragua, Honduras, El Salvador, and Guatemala, and militarism is still spreading. Of these, only Peru has a progressive regime.

But, largely because of Dr. Kissinger himself, international affairs are no longer guided by ideology. So Latin America's real problems—its economic problems—are now the determining factors in any new relationship with Washington. And the concept that these problems can be resolved without a reordering—and perhaps a convulsion—of the world economy is as outdated as a reliance on ideology.

But at the human level, at the subsistence level at which most—yes, most—Latin Americans live, what does this mean? Dare one say, nothing? The former foreign minister of Venezuela, Dr. Aristides Calvani, liked to compare the battle of developing countries to the struggle of the trade unions in nineteenth-century England. "The oil producers are merely the first trade union," he said. "But with courage and short-term sacrifice, the producers of other raw materials can help build a massive trade union movement of developing nations."

The analogy is interesting and appropriate, but what about the real trade union movements of Latin America—will the benefits of any world economic reform seep down to the poor workers and peasants of each country? The case of the Arab oil producers offers no encouragement. In Venezuela the oil wealth is also concentrated in a few hands. In many cases, in fact, new wealth will merely strengthen right-wing and repressive regimes. . . . In Ecuador, which became an oil exporter in 1972, an unpopular military regime already has been saved by increased oil revenues.

According to Washington's new policy toward the continent, all this is irrelevant. Its rather special "hands-off" policy—noninterference in the internal affairs of right-wing dictatorships—ensures that poverty will remain widespread even if raw-material prices rise sharply.

But the US influence—political, economic, and cultural—is enormous even without a policy of rapprochement in Washington. The economic shadow is obvious. Trade between the regions in 1973 exceeded $16.5 billion—$1.8 billion to the advantage of the US—and US private investment in the continent approached $18 billion. In some smaller countries a single US company dominates the entire local economy. US businessmen are not reluctant to express and promote their preferences in local politics, too.

Culturally, US companies provide most of the entertainment and information available in the continent—films, television, and wire-service news. Local US-owned subsidiaries also bring with them a special consumer consciousness that eventually distorts local tastes to conform with the American Dream.

On critical occasions, the US, of course, intervenes directly in local affairs. But its indirect political influence is perhaps even more important. Events in the US are followed and are reported closely in Latin America. The "demonstration effect" is powerful, and political unrest in the US is quickly reflected in Latin America. For example, upheavals in Latin America during the sixties cannot be separated from the antiwar movement in the US at the same time.

Thus, even without an interventionist policy, the US, by its very nature, cannot avoid intervening as a domestic political factor in every Latin American country. So, once again, the basic power relationship should not be obscured by conferences and declarations. Change will probably come to Latin America some time after it has reached the US.

IN A WORLD CONTEXT [4]

Latin America can be perceived as the less modernized segment of the Western world. The more common practice, to be sure, is to think of Latin America as sharing basic characteristics with Africa and Asia, and to conceive of these three large areas as the less developed world. While the central problem facing Latin America today is social and economic transformation, its level of economic development sets Latin America apart from Africa and much of Asia, and its historical tradition links it more closely to the West....

The average per capita income of Latin America is over three times that of Africa and Asia. Per capita GNP [gross national product] of a half dozen of the larger Latin American countries is not far from the level of some advanced countries, such as Austria, Finland, Italy, Japan or the Netherlands, after World War II. Latin America is more industrialized than Africa and Asia. Over 25 percent of GNP for the region as a whole originates from industry. By this measure also, Latin America is approaching a degree

[4] From *Forces for Change in Latin America: U.S. Policy Implications*, by Colin I. Bradford, Jr., official of the Organization of American States. Overseas Development Council. 1717 Massachusetts Ave. N.W. Washington, D.C. 20036. '71. p 3-9. Reprinted by permission.

of development reached by some advanced countries after the last world war.

But Latin America is also the area with the highest rates of population growth and urbanization in the world. Population growth in Latin America has been generally twice that of the more developed regions during the last fifty years. Currently, over 50 percent of the total population in the area live in cities, as compared to 25 percent for all low income regions together. Buenos Aires, Mexico City, Rio de Janeiro, and São Paulo are among the fifteen largest cities in the world. By the end of the century, 80 percent of Latin America's total population will be urbanized, an average equal to the more advanced regions.

While the rate of urbanization in Latin America parallels that of more developed areas of the world, economic development has neither the means of absorbing this urban population into the active labor force, nor the dynamism to generate adequate incomes for those remaining in agriculture. Despite rates of economic growth which are impressive in comparison with comparable periods of development in Europe and North America, the structure and dynamism of Latin American economies are insufficient, relative to population, to satisfy the needs and demands of the majority of Latin Americans. The economies are unable to provide the distribution of goods, services, and jobs the broad mass of people in Latin America require. This imbalance between the population and the economic system will be at the heart of the development problem in Latin America in the years ahead.

The developed nations, particularly the US, have an important role. Many of the outstanding problems of this hemisphere are those which spring from disparities of power within and between nations. The productive power, growing markets and economic dynamism of the developed economies are the overwhelming determinants of the world economic system. There is a great sense in Latin America of being unable to control or influence these forces which determine major aspects of economic life. The problem of "dependence" in its economic, social, political and cultural sense has been, and continues to be, a major preoccupation of intellectuals, social scientists, and, to an increasing extent, policy makers in Latin America.

Latin America's development problem is inextricably linked to Latin America's economic relationship to the rest of the world. External dependence in trade, technology and capital is at the center of economic underdevelopment both in conceptual terms and in day-to-day decision making. To a very great extent national development policies in Latin America are based on both obstacles and opportunities in the international economic environment.

A long-standing problem is that this importance to Latin America of the world economy and of policies in the developed countries is not matched by the low priority accorded to Latin America in the foreign policy of the US. Because of its proximity to the US and because of the common basis of Western tradition, there has been a tendency among some to think of Latin America as having a "special relationship" with the US. Those who argue that Latin America is of critical importance to the security of the United States believe that Latin America should receive "high priority" status in US foreign economic policy.

But the fact is that North American investment and trade concentrates on the developed countries. Low-income countries per se do not receive high policy attention. For the US policy maker Latin America does not loom large in the scale of power, however important the US may be to his Latin American counterpart.

This disparity between the importance of the US in Latin America, and the relative unimportance of Latin America to the US, means that the attention given to the area by the US is not commensurate with the effects of US power in Latin America. US policies do not appear to Latin Americans to reflect a consciousness of the enormous effect of the US in the region. This tends to fan the flames of resentment in Latin America and complicate US-Latin American relations in both political and economic matters. Even if adequate attention were given to Latin America, the problems would not be easily resolved. Still, if US policy makers were to begin to focus on the implications of US power in the region and the appropriateness of US trade, investment and aid to the Latin American political context, it could be the beginning of better relations in the Western Hemisphere. Renewed attention to US relations with Latin America can instill creative changes in foreign policy by adapting US economic relations to new realities and by generating a responsive attitude to positive political changes in Latin America.

The Use of Power in Latin America

Increasingly the problem of development in Latin America revolves around the problem of power disparities. There is not only a disparity of wealth between rich and poor but a sharp contrast in power between large social groups. In Latin America the disparities in income result from the historic failure of the economic systems to incorporate the broad mass of Latin Americans. However, these are only the economic aspects of systems of power relations that ascribe influence, ownership and social prestige to relatively small elites and exclude the majority from access to the instruments of power.

Until recently the predominance of traditional elites was the source of social cohesion and control. With the revolution in communications, the values and authority of Latin American elites have been increasingly challenged by a growing self-awareness of majority groups in Latin America: the *campesinos* [farm workers], urban workers, slum dwellers and unemployed. These social groups are now assertive where they once were passive acceptors of the status quo. There is growing outrage and alienation from systems of power relations which not only seem to fail to satisfy their material needs but also do not represent their values or respond to their political demands. The economic rise of the middle class in many Latin American countries and their access to power have resulted from economic growth rather than from deliberate political programs to open the system to include low-income groups. Now, social tensions and political consciousness have grown to the point that new leaders can gain political power through efforts to deal with the conditions of those historically without power.

With these emerging pressures and realities, development increasingly means the transformation of power relations from a closed, elitist system to an open, mass-oriented society. The problem of development has become in essence a problem of the use and control of power. The political question of who shall rule, and for whom, is the most fundamental in looking ahead to Latin America's future.

The conflict between the still powerful traditional elites and the majority is increasingly polarized in Latin America. On the one hand, the traditional groups tend to be wedded to the notion that the central problem is economic growth and that an accelerated rate of growth will lead to incorporation of the previously excluded segments of society. Their concept is that the social conditions of the popular class do not require attention per se but will be resolved as the economy as a whole grows more rapidly. They appear to be committed to the economic expansion of the system as it is, and opposed to significant structural transformation. The traditional elites are internationalist in outlook and receptive to technology and consumer values originating from abroad. They see no particular conflict between foreign investment and national sovereignty. They see the role of the state as one of providing the infrastructure necessary for private-sector growth, rather than intervening directly in productive activities. Their own economic enterprises are frequently oriented toward maximizing per unit profits within a limited market, rather than maximizing total profits through large volume as is the orientation of the new entrepreneurial class.

On the other hand, the majority is increasingly pressing for policies which deal directly with economic and social inequities. The advocates of these policies tend to be emergent groups within the church and the military, among youth, the technocrats and the democratic Left. Political support is found among the increasingly urbanized and aware low-income groups. They ask for change in the representative structure of institutions, opening decision-making processes to all segments of society, not just those with economic power. An essential element of these policies is change in ownership and management structure in industrial and agricultural enterprises to include worker participation. A major goal is the transformation of the economic structure to achieve a new, more equitable economic order independent of the control of the traditional elite or of foreign investment. These groups believe the state is the only source of focused power sufficient to confront the traditional elite and potent external forces. Hence, a major role is seen for the state in industrialization, in defining "rules of the game" for domestic and foreign private investors, and in the formulation of a development strategy for achievement of a new economic order.

This conflict in political vision and policy outlook between the traditional elites and the majority is leading to tension throughout the hemisphere. In Colombia, for example, the two major elite parties have shared power in a National Front government since 1958, when they took over a chaotic economic tangle left by General Rojas Pinilla. Despite some enlightened presidential leadership in the intervening years, the National Front was severely challenged in the 1970 elections by the seventy-year-old general. Of the more than 4 million votes cast in the presidential elections in April 1970, the National Front candidate, Misael Pastrana, prevailed over Rojas Pinilla by a mere 64,000 votes. Much of Pinilla's support comes from the low-income sectors of the electorate. His surprising showing can be seen as a measure of the frustration of the popular classes with the pace of change under an elitist reform government.

Similarly, in Chile the election in September 1970, clearly showed a majority support for policies of structural transformation. The combined votes for the victorious Salvador Allende, a Socialist, and Radomiro Tomic, a leftist Christian Democrat, constituted two thirds of the total vote. This is particularly significant coming, as it does, on the heels of six years of Christian Democrat Eduardo Frei Montalva's presidency, the most reform-motivated democratic government in the hemisphere. [Allende's government was overthrown in 1973 and replaced by a military dictatorship. See "The Bloody End of a Marxist Dream," in Section IV, below.—Ed.]

Peru illustrates the most interesting case of elite-majority conflict. In October of 1968 the left wing of the military seized power from democratically elected President Fernando Belaunde Terry for having entered into an agreement with Standard Oil of New Jersey—an arrangement which they considered to be in violation of national sovereignty. The new military government, under General Juan Velasco Alvarado, immediately nationalized the Standard Oil industrial complex. . . . Since then, major new legislative measures have been promulgated by the government regarding agrarian reform, industry, mining, and banking. These laws are intended to reshape economic relations to satisfy new priorities for national sovereignty and the redistribution of power.

These events in Colombia, Chile and Peru reflect the growing pressures for changes in Latin America. . . . Brazil has achieved spectacular rates of growth in recent years while at the same time repression has been used to control opposition groups. In the larger countries, then, there is a tendency toward more conservative governments and a narrower focus on economic growth to the exclusion of distribution measures. While the claims on the political systems in Latin America for economic change appear to be pervasive and increasing, the modes of dealing with these pressures differ as between the larger countries and those along the Andean chain. This translates the tension between the forces for change and those favoring the status quo into international dimensions, creating divergences between nations within the region.

Hence, as we look ahead one of the major questions is what types of governments will evolve in Latin America. Pressures challenge the capacity of institutions to absorb and control emerging problems. The mechanism of compromise is increasingly difficult to employ as major social groups are associated with fundamentally conflicting sets of interests and even opposed value systems. Measures which satisfy one group are anathema to another. In this context, governments find it difficult to permit the free flow of interests and pressures to come to bear on policy decisions. Governments are unable to remain aloof, absorbing and adjudicating interests in a detached manner. Increasingly they find themselves directly involved in the issues of social conflict.

To govern in this context increasingly means to be opposed. This opposition undermines the capacity of governments to deliver, even for the groups they purport to represent. Faced with pressures from both constituents and the opposition, there is a tendency to resort to force. The roots of contemporary authoritarianism in Latin America are in this social context of politics.

Hence, political systems in Latin America are under enormous pressure arising from a new consciousness of major social groups. Much of this pressure is due to a conflict in values between those who have traditionally exercised power in Latin America and those with very little power at all. Increasingly those without power are gaining a greater voice within the political systems of the region, often through new types of political leaders or different types of government.

In the past Latin American political systems, regardless

of political form, reflected the existing power structure, giving greater leverage to the rich than to the poor. In such
systems frequently the interests which are the most influential are those which are the least representative. The fact
that this has often been the case may, in part, account for
the disappearance of democratic governments in many Latin
American countries in recent years. The new advocates of
the popular majority—whether leftist politicians, military or
church leaders—find it difficult to gain access to power
within the existing political forms and, once in power, to
carry out a development design which is at odds with the
interests of economic power groups.

Hence, as the questions of who rules and for whom increasingly turn toward greater representation of majority
interest, Latin American political systems will adopt new
molds. These new forms may not always be of a constitutional nature. This trend is reenforced not only by the
struggle for power but also by the conflicts of values and
interests which result from any effort to achieve structural
transformation. These conflicts cripple compromise and consensus as procedures of governance.

Thus a substantial degree of abrogation of democratic
processes and a certain measure of authoritarianism seems
nearly inevitable as we look ahead. In the past, the fre-
quency of coups and dictatorships reflected competition
among elites as to who would rule for the elites as a whole.
Today, political instability and authoritarianism in Latin
America, including the emergence of the military as a mechanism for governance, reflects the increasing demand for
social change. Elites continue to compete for power but the
base of representation has widened. Different elites now
represent decidedly different political programs; this makes
it difficult for the group in power to remain open to the influence and opposition of those out of power. This is a relatively new development.

Depending upon who is in power, these tendencies may
indeed result in governments that are more representative

of the great majority of people than might be the case with a more strict adherence to present constitutional or democratic procedures. The extent to which this is so, the degree to which authoritarianism leads to repression, and the openness or closedness of governments to the world community may be affected by the policies of the developed nations.

These factors challenge the flexibility and adaptability of American foreign policy. An element in US foreign policy has been the support of the US for democratically elected regimes abroad. In some instances, this commitment has superseded US dedication to development: when faced with a choice between aiding a democratic government with fairly traditional economic policies and a nondemocratic government with a strong development orientation, the former has been more attractive. Social consciousness and pressure are at such a stage in Latin America that democratic governments with traditional economic policies now find it difficult to survive. Also, the meaning of development now goes beyond economic growth to the transformation of power relations. In these circumstances the pressure for economic democracy is greater than the pressure for political democracy. The legitimacy of governments increasingly rests on their effectiveness in promoting economic change and development, and less upon the degree to which the transfer of power occurs with the consent of the governed. Increasingly, events will force the US to choose between its commitment to democracy and its concern for the social conditions of the low-income Latin American masses. This poses a fundamental dilemma for American foreign policy toward Latin America in the 1970s.

The Effect of the Power of the World Economy

A key element affecting the Latin American mix of policies is the US. Foreign economic relations, particularly with the US, are interlaced with domestic development policies through the intricacies of economics. In addition, there is the overwhelming fact of the enormous power of the US in the Western Hemisphere.

The glaring internal disparities in power relations in Latin America are aggravated by the enormous gap in power between the national governments of Latin America and the major forces of the world economy. The global forces behind world trade, investment, and financial flows tend to swamp efforts to control national destiny, just when nationalism is on the rise. These international economic forces tend to impinge on the capacity of national governments in the Western Hemisphere to assert controlling decision-making power in economic matters. Since much of this external economic power seems to emanate from the US, these forces appear particularly threatening to Latin American leaders.

If the drive for development in Latin America were solely a matter of economic growth, the spread of American economic power in the world might be less subject to question. To a large extent, however, economic development is not seen as an end in itself in Latin America. Instead many Latin Americans feel that the ultimate goal of development in Latin America is the strengthening of the nation as an autonomous entity. . . .

Nationalism in Latin America is seen as a channel through which independence of economic power can function. Will for independence, search for identity, determination to control resources, the faculty to transform intentions into actions, the will for power—these are all deeply Western values. Their realization in Latin America is identified with the nation-state. To the extent that economic forces emanating from the US erode and are perceived to debilitate the possibilities for Latin Americans to realize these values, they work against the system of values which we Americans share with the people of Latin America.

SUDDENLY IT'S MAÑANA IN LATIN AMERICA [5]

Even when our emissaries to Latin America are being stoned in the streets, communiqués out of the State Department refer to hemispheric "solidarity" and the pursuit of democratic development and social progress. This sort of fog makes it hard to perceive major changes in inter-American relations. Yet beneath a large amount of only slightly altered rhetoric, the past year has been a time of significant change indeed.

As important producers of commodities that were suddenly in short supply, the Latin Americans saw their export earnings soar and found their economic power considerably enhanced. They began to use their natural resources to drive harder bargains with the industrial world. They served notice that they will try to keep commodity prices propped up high, and they opened a campaign for better access to the US market for their rapidly growing exports of manufactured goods as well. With a new self-confidence born of unaccustomed prosperity, they also discarded or fundamentally revised some of the major tenets of their postwar foreign policy.

In a series of meetings behind closed doors . . . Latin America's foreign ministers concluded that the concept of a Western Hemisphere "community" of states, though enshrined in solemn treaties, is a diplomatic fiction that has outlived its usefulness. Politically, they say, the US-led community has become another relic of the cold war. As an economic concept, it presupposes a considerable mutuality of interests, when in fact the US is usually on one side of the bargaining table and the Latin Americans are on the other. . . .

[5] From article by Richard Armstrong, writer on world affairs. *Fortune.* 90:138-43+. Ag. '74. Reprinted by permission.

Retrieving Their Proxies

This fundamental change has attracted much more attention in Latin America than in the US, where the "new dialogue" with our neighbors has generally been described as another personal triumph for Kissinger. [See "Kissinger's 'New Dialogue,'" in this section, above.] Certainly he was very warmly received, but behind the closed doors, the meetings were more notable for candor than affection. At . . . [a session in Mexico City in February 1974], Kissinger began talking in traditional terms about the inter-American community. "He provoked a very harsh reaction," says Enrique Bernstein, the senior career diplomat in Chile's Ministry of Foreign Relations. "The Latin Americans said how can you have a 'community' that includes a rich, powerful country like the US, with worldwide commitments, and underdeveloped countries like ours?"

The Mexico City communiqué declared that inter-American relations must be based on "respect for the right of countries to choose their own political, economic, and social systems," and it recognized that the countries have "different approaches on foreign policy." In a follow-up decision at Washington, Kissinger agreed that the US would not try to block an invitation to Cuba to attend a meeting of the foreign ministers in Buenos Aires next year. The US also agreed to allow General Motors, Ford, and Chrysler subsidiaries in Argentina to sell forty thousand cars and trucks to Cuba as part of an Argentine state trading deal. The Latin Americans pressed for these changes in policy, as a Brazilian diplomat explains, not because they are turning to the Left, but because "nobody is handing out proxies anymore for the US to conduct their foreign affairs."

Reluctant Cold Warriors

While the issues themselves may seem mostly symbolic to Americans, they reflect deep fears among Latin Americans about US interference with their sovereignty. When the

Latin Americans ratified the founding documents of the postwar system—the Reciprocal Assistance Treaty, signed in Rio in 1947, and the OAS [Organization of American States] charter a year later—they did so mainly to have guarantees against the use of armed intervention by the US. But at a meeting of the OAS in Caracas in 1954, they found themselves enlisted in the cold war in return for promises of aid, a turning point they later came to regret.

The US was covertly preparing to sponsor a revolution that was to topple a left-wing government in Guatemala. John Foster Dulles [secretary of state during the Eisenhower Administration], the master bloc-builder, secured passage of a resolution declaring that control of any American government by the Communists constituted a threat to the hemisphere within the meaning of the Rio treaty. Eight years later the treaty was invoked to kick Cuba out of the OAS, and two years after that to impose economic sanctions. February's Mexico City communiqué was specifically aimed at repudiating the Dulles resolution. And the Argentine-Cuban deal knocks a hole in the blockade, "well, big enough to drive a truck through," a Mexican diplomat quips.

The Latin Americans have never been very happy with their quid pro quo for joining the cold war. Quite a lot of aid has flowed south over the years, but most of it was tied to the purchase of US products and accompanied by political conditions that skittered about according to the persuasions of the particular Administration in power in Washington. The Latin Americans were told in the 1950s to balance their budgets and let private enterprise do the development job, and they were told in the days of John F. Kennedy's Alliance for Progress that they must redistribute the wealth and the land.

In a careful study called *The Alliance That Lost Its Way*, Juan De Onís of the New York *Times* and Jerome Levinson, a lawyer who was with the Agency for International Development, conclude that the Alliance was so schizoid in its pursuit of both "social justice" and development that it failed to accomplish much in either respect. Construction of new schools and housing did not even keep up with increases in the population, and economic growth rates remained almost flat during the 1960s.

The Army Came at Midnight

When Kennedy officials used to warn that "it is one minute until midnight in Latin America," they meant that the Communists were about to take over. But when midnight came for five of the countries—Brazil, Bolivia, Peru, Uruguay, and Chile—it was primarily because of mismanagement by the democratic Left. And it was the army rather than Communists that appeared at the presidential palace to take over the receivership in bankruptcy. Today only Costa Rica, Colombia, Venezuela, and perhaps Argentina could be considered functioning democracies. . . .

Their sobering experience with visionary reforms has convinced the Latin American leadership that growth must come first. When Kissinger told the foreign ministers in Mexico that they would be lucky if present aid levels are maintained, nobody bothered to protest. "The welfare days are just about over," says a Brazilian diplomat with a shrug. While a number of countries are spending more heavily than ever for education, other Alliance goals such as "decent homes for all our people" have been scaled down to the possible: housing banks to finance homes for workers who can meet mortgage payments, and modest self-help programs in the wretched shantytowns that ring Latin America's major cities. The Latin Americans figure that they can pay for these modest social programs themselves, for they see, at long last, the possibility of sustained economic growth.

It would be difficult to overestimate the impact of the recent commodity boom on the Latin American leadership. Major exports such as copper, oil, coffee, sugar, and beef have been in extremely strong demand. Exports increased 36 percent . . . [in 1973], to $23 billion. Brazil scored a 55 percent gain. Foreign-exchange reserves rose by 62 percent, to $14 billion—a transfer of capital far exceeding any-thing even dreamed of in the years of the Alliance.

Whatever the immediate trend in commodity prices . . . the Latin Americans believe that the terms of trade have turned decisively in favor of raw-materials producers after running the other way for most of the last thirty years. And Latin America is a storehouse of natural wealth that has not even been fully explored. Shigeaki Ueki, Brazil's Minister of Mines and Energy, says: "You will understand that the hunt has barely begun when I tell you that last year in the interior we found a river one thousand kilometers long that we didn't even know existed." Latin America's proven oil reserves are unevenly distributed, but the region is a net exporter of petroleum, and the major producer, Venezuela, has promised to be a banker to its poorer neighbors. The threat of world food shortages has called attention to Latin America's most neglected resource of all, an abundance of tillable tropical land. . . .

Forays Outside the Walls

Partly by taking advantage of their new economic muscle in commodities, the Latin Americans expect to become major exporters of finished manufactured goods as well. The planners are not entirely clear about how it can be done, but they intend to use their abundance of the one to open mar-kets for the other, possibly through state trading deals. In-deed, Latin America's exports of manufactured goods are already growing rapidly, as a result of a fundamental change in development strategies.

When the Latin American countries first went hell-bent for industrialization in the years after World War II, the original aim was to make at home what they had been im-porting—mainly consumer goods. These industries had no trouble flourishing behind high tariff walls, but they con-tinue to require a lot of imported machinery and compo-nents, and production runs were usually too small to be efficient. "Even our pharmaceutical plants are nothing but pill assembly lines," complains Rear Admiral Jiménez de Lucio, Peru's minister of industry and tourism.

In time, a certain amount of disillusion set in. "By the late 1960s," says Dragoslav Avramovic, the chief economist for Latin America at the World Bank, "the leadership had fully grasped that lack of foreign exchange was the key constraint on development, and a major reallocation of resources was made to increase exports."

Is Uncle Sam Unkind to Flower Girls?

The beneficiaries of this drive were the most efficient local industries—for example Colombian textiles, Mexican steel, and Brazilian autos. To push them into markets abroad, the governments used such hidden subsidies as preferential exchange rates or rebates on local taxes. At first, says Avramovic, the Latin Americans were suspicious of encouraging expanded output of primary products. They were afraid of driving down prices, as had happened so often in the past. "But as the terms of trade improved," Avramovic says, "they saw they could increase exports of both primary and manufactured goods."

When the drive for exports runs into import barriers in the US, the collision can make the sort of headlines that used to be reserved for political interference by the US in Latin American affairs. Few Americans are aware that Colombia shipped us $8 million worth of cut flowers . . . [in 1973] or even that Brazil shipped us $81 million worth of shoes, much less that both of these product lines have run into difficulties lately with the US tariff authorities. But for Colombians and Brazilians these are important issues. The high feeling in Colombia about cut flowers was captured by a Bogotá newspaper a few months ago in a cartoon that showed Uncle Sam scowling at a little flower girl in a tattered dress.

Colombia's cut-flower producers, as exporters of "nontraditional" products, get government bonds equal to 15 percent of export sales, and the Brazilian shoemakers get a tax rebate amounting to as much as 30 percent of sales. American producers of competing products charge that these incentives amount to an export "bounty" in violation of the Tariff Act of 1930. There is truth to the charge, but it it also true that almost every country subsidizes exports in either obvious or unobvious ways.

"These are difficult cases," sighs a Brazil-based US diplomat, who points out that they raise questions applicable to all of Latin America's export-support programs. "The shoe industry is a terrific success story here. It was created by a bunch of small entrepreneurs down in Porto Alegre. They work from US lasts and stay on top of new fashions. Brazil's leather exports have declined because the leather is going out as shoes. Sales to the US doubled last year. We ran a lot of AID [Agency for International Development] programs trying to encourage the underdeveloped countries to upgrade their exports in exactly this way."

The Latin Americans know that, whatever the letter of the law, most trade decisions in the US are arrived at through a process of political give-and-take. And so they have been hammering away at Kissinger about shoes and flowers and so on. "He seemed surprised that we spent so much time talking trade rather than politics," says an Argentine diplomat. But the Latin Americans are deeply concerned because they have run a trade deficit with the US in most of the years since World War II. It came to $1.3 billion . . . [in 1973]. . . .

Integration With the World

The outstanding exception to this trend is Brazil, which has been doing so well lately it hardly needs Kissinger's help at all. Brazil has extended a warm welcome to US corporations, a strategy that is described in its Five Year Plan as "integrating Brazil into the world economy." The shoemakers of Porto Alegre have had to fend for themselves, but most of Brazil's sales of manufactured goods abroad are handled by multinational corporations. In many cases they agree to fulfill informal export quotas to earn foreign exchange. Unsurprisingly, Ford expects to have no trouble finding a market abroad for automobile engines, nor does IBM Brazil lack customers for computer hardware.

The Brazilian approach and the more nationalistic development model have quite different implications for future US relationships with Latin America. The Brazilian-style drive for a larger share of the US market will be beneficial for both sides. In the other case, the US is being told, in effect, that its share of the economic benefit from the relationship will be reduced because its bargaining position has weakened. So far at least, the friendlier of the two models is also the more successful.

Brazil is impelled by its vision of one day joining the ranks of the world's great powers. . . . It has elevated economic pragmatism to the status of a state religion, with the planners as priests. They are presiding over an intense process of capital creation. Because profits are extremely high and are being reinvested, savings by businesses and individuals amounted to 23 percent of the gross national product last year, compared with 15 percent in the US. That doesn't count the billions more the government takes out of the economy in consumer taxes and pours back into infrastructure, or the $3.7 billion in foreign capital that came in last year. . . .

Brazil's powerful economic boom is now in its ninth year. By the end of 1974 it will have doubled the gross national product, to $60 billion. Manufacturing has been growing by 14 percent a year, and just about every major multinational corporation is taking part. Already exporting 62,000 cars a year, Volkswagen is expanding in São Paulo while cutting production in Germany. Fiat is putting in a $300 million plant near Belo Horizonte. Ishikawajima-Harima will build supertankers at its shipyard in Rio. Dow Chemical is adding $100 million in new petro-chemical capacity. And the list goes on and on. . . .

But it is what's happening in agriculture that demonstrates most dramatically the wallop private enterprise can have when propelled by credit and tax incentives. Corporations can get cut-rate loans for farming, and they are entitled to deduct approved investments from their taxable income. Consequently they have been rushing to bring modern agribusiness methods to Brazil's immense virgin lands. Agricultural production increased 19 percent by physical volume and doubled in value just within the last three years.

Agronomists disagree as to how far north toward the equatorial rain belt farming can be pushed. But US shipping tycoon Daniel K. Ludwig ... has been experimenting with both row crops and cattle on 3.5 million acres deep in the Amazon basin, where torrential rainfalls make erosion a formidable problem. Volkswagen has just bought 300,000 acres for a cattle ranch in the basin. . . .

"One Nation Divided"

Perhaps Brazil's greatest advantage is simply its size—and the self-confident pride that size makes possible. All by itself, the country is a common market of 104 million people. By contrast, the leaders of Spanish America ... describe themselves as "one nation divided." They are working toward a common market and are almost obsessed by fears that the multinational corporations may somehow grab the juiciest portions of it. They regard American companies in particular as a threat to their cultural identity. . . .

Besides expropriating big US holdings, the Spanish Americans have been writing laws designed to force other US companies to sell a majority interest to local investors. They think that if US companies don't care to play under those tough rules, their Japanese or European competitors will. In other words, while Brazil is using the lure of profits to attract the capital it needs, the other countries are threatening US companies with loss of position in markets where they have been entrenched. At stake are investments that yield profit remittances of around a billion dollars a year.

In one field, at least, the Spanish American countries have been able to write their own tickets. Mining presents the confusing spectacle of countries expropriating existing concessions in the interests of "national sovereignty" and then signing new contracts, often with the very same companies, to open up additional production. Under the new contracts, the government is usually the majority owner of the project, and while this is not necessarily any more profitable than collecting royalties, it is a lot more palatable politically.

In Peru, the expropriation of the Cerro de Pasco copper mines by the leftist military government was bitterly contested, and agreement on compensation was not reached until the US sent down a special emissary . . . [in 1973]. But Cerro is partners with the three other US companies, including American Smelting & Refining, in the Southern Peru Copper Company, which is investing $550 million in a new mine. It will increase Peru's copper production by about two thirds, to 360,000 tons a year. Under a profit-sharing plan, the mine workers will eventually own half the company. Peru also expropriated the International Petroleum Company (an Exxon subsidiary) and never paid for it. Nonetheless, twenty American companies are looking for oil in the Amazon jungle and offshore as partners of the Peruvian government.

A Different Set of Judgments

The military junta in Chile intends to hang on to the copper mines seized by the late President Salvador Allende, but it is looking for help in opening new ones. Venezuela will expropriate the big iron-ore concessions held by Bethlehem and US Steel and nationalize the oil fields sometime soon. But the government is expected to hire foreign companies, probably the ones already there, to pump the old oil and look for new.

Remarkable as it may seem to other businessmen, taking those lumps and coming back for more is part of the game for oil and mining men. They do so because the payout, when they succeed, is swift and large. They have learned to live with partnership deals in other parts of the world, such as Indonesia. And the minerals are worth far more than they were a few years ago.

In other enterprises, however, a different set of investment judgments apply. The immediate effect of those tough new terms has been to scare new capital away from most of the Spanish American countries. This could cripple a lot of development plans.

The companies already established in these countries face an uncertain future. For example, the six members of the Andean Pact—Chile, Peru, Bolivia, Ecuador, Colombia, and Venezuela—are pledged by treaty to achieve a common market by 1985, and they have declared such fields as banking, insurance, and domestic trade off limits to foreign companies. But the application of this rule to existing companies can only be described as capricious; some are being forced to sell out, and others are not. Foreign manufacturing companies will be denied access to the common market and to local credit. While some of the multinationals are shopping around for local partners, most of them are hanging on for now and trying to fathom the Andean Pact's baffling new limit on profit remittances, which is being variously interpreted by the six governments.

Later on, a much larger common market is supposed to encompass the Andean Pact, the five-member Central American Common Market, and the rest of Latin America as well. The benefits of this market, too, are to be reserved for locally controlled companies.

Nationalizing Sopranos

As the tariff walls come down, Argentina, the most developed country of them all, plans to become a major exporter of manufactures to its neighbors. And the new government seems likely to hold to the views of the late Juan Perón, who was noted as a high-spirited Argentina

Firster. . . . [In 1973] the Peronistas canceled the contracts
of foreign opera singers to make room for Argentine war-
blers. Having condemned the proud old Teatro Colón in
Buenos Aires to its worst season in living memory, they
went on . . . to pass a foreign-investment code that limits
remittances of profits and royalties to 12.5 percent on in-
vested capital. That is not a handsome return in a country
where foreign executives run the risk of being kidnaped or
murdered. . . .

All of these countries are actively seeking European and
Japanese capital to make up for the falloff in US investment.
Japan is now Mexico's third-largest trading partner (after
the US and West Germany), and to save money on shipping
costs the Japanese are putting up $45 million to finance the
construction of an ultramodern port at Manzanillo, west of
Mexico City. In Argentina, Fiat has shot past its American
competitors to become the largest foreign enterprise in the
country.

The leftist military regime in Peru, after expropriating
a number of American companies, used a loophole in the
Andean Pact to give a local monopoly in petrochemicals to
Bayer and another in diesel engines to a jointly owned subsidiary of Volvo and Britain's Perkins Engines. In each
case, the foreigners have 70 percent control. The loophole
is that when the Andean governments go into business on
their own hook, they can offer handsomer terms. Peru declared petrochemicals and diesel engines "strategic industries," which means that the companies won't have to pay
out stock to their workers as other Peruvian companies
must do.

US investment in Latin America—$18 billion at book
value, of which $3 billion is in Brazil—still far surpasses
the total from all of Europe and Japan combined. Statistics
on non-US investment are five years out of date, but the
current figure is probably less than $8 billion. It is increas-
ing rapidly, however, and the very fact that the Europeans
and Japanese are latecomers to the area gives them a valu-

able freedom of maneuver: they can tailor their deals to the prevailing political climate.

Most US companies have no objection in principle to joint ventures; they have gone into a lot of them in countries around the world, including Brazil and Mexico. They concede that the joint venture is the pattern of the future in Latin America. But they have built up their stakes over many years and don't care to sell 51 percent interests at bankruptcy prices. An American manager in Buenos Aires says he doubts whether there is enough venture capital in all Argentina to pay fair value for control of the DuPont subsidiary (worth more than $100 million), much less all the rest. In many countries, partners who could be counted on to give skillful direction to the enterprise are even scarcer than capital.

Cheers for the Brazilian Version

As US executives see it, the crucial competition in the years ahead will be the contest between Latin America's two very different approaches to development. Naturally enough, they will be cheering for the Brazilian version. If Brazil's boom continues, they say, neighboring countries will feel tremendous pressure to try to match the results by copying the methods.

The manager of a big American subsidiary in Buenos Aires mentions that thousands of technicians from Argentina and other Spanish American countries now work in São Paulo. "The tremendous pool of talent we used to be able to call on here is now over in Brazil," he says, "and the point hasn't been lost on the Argentine government." If foreign capital won't come in under those new investment laws, then the prideful countries of Spanish America may in time change the laws.

In private conversations, Henry Kissinger has admitted candidly that these large US interests are a major reason for his efforts to improve relations. US subsidiaries abroad not only remit profits but also are major customers for US exports. So what is bad for the companies is bad for the US balance of payments.

But the US must also consider its strategic interest in having friendly neighbors, whatever their development policies. However strongly US executives may express their preference for the Brazilian as opposed to the other development model, Kissinger has been careful to avoid playing favorites, or coming across as an agent of US capitalism. At ... [a meeting in Washington in April 1974] he gave his support to a favorite Latin project: a special committee to study the behavior of the multinationals. (The Latin Americans are particularly interested in finding out whether the companies use bookkeeping devices to escape taxes.) ...

The High Cost of Cheap Steaks

Kissinger has tried, politely, to prod the Latin Americans into paying more attention to agriculture, a field where Brazil is almost alone in taking vigorous advantage of the new opportunities. In most Latin American countries, building a road to open new farmlands would be a far better use of scarce resources than expropriating foreign companies. But out of a naive preference for industry, the governments have consistently shortchanged the agriculture, even while deploring the predictable result: a mass migration of peasants to the urban slums.

An even bigger problem than the lack of roads or other agricultural infrastructure is the fact that food prices are controlled almost everywhere for the benefit of city dwellers. But the prices are set so low that farmers cannot afford the fertilizer and other inputs needed to increase production. ...

The Right to Ride a Tiger

Latin leaders say there will still be a "special relationship" with the US in economic terms, if only because of proximity. ... They don't want to abrogate the Rio treaty, which has been useful in settling border disputes, although they do want to amend the treaty and the OAS charter to recognize that a "plurality of ideologies" may coexist in the Americas. In plain words, they insist on their right to go socialist or even Communist if they choose.

They intend to press Kissinger on trade matters . . . but it will be surprising if Kissinger has much to give. . . . Moreover, Latin Americans consider our nontariff barriers, such as quotas or the uneven enforcement of sanitary regulations for food products, to be an even bigger problem than tariffs. . . .

In the Latin American view, Kissinger, by agreeably amending the inter-American system to fit their prescription, has taken a clever, subtle tack. Through scrapping cold-war policies that the US had lost interest in anyway, they say, he sought to revitalize the Alliance and detach Latin America somewhat from the rest of the Third World of commodity-producing countries.

The Latin Americans nonetheless intend to follow their own economic interests. "After the Arabs, we will all be flexing our muscles," says an Argentine diplomat. Producer countries have already raised prices for bananas and bauxite. Chile and Peru are conferring with Zambia and Zaïre to see what might be done in copper. The Argentines talk about long-term barter deals and even "denying Latin American markets" to US goods. The Brazilians, who like to compete, are skeptical of market-rigging schemes, but they seek the same goals as their neighbors. All of the Latin Americans have come to appreciate that in unity there is strength.

II. THE COUNTRIES OF SOUTH AMERICA

EDITOR'S INTRODUCTION

This section presents articles on a number of South American countries to highlight their current major problems and characteristics. The object is not only to sketch the present scene in these countries, but to show them in such a way as to give the reader a feeling for the differences among them.

The first article deals with Argentina and the prime phenomenon in that country's life—its late leader, Juan Perón. In many respects, he was to his people what President Franklin D. Roosevelt had been to Americans during the depression of the 1930s and World War II—a man who they believed could guide them from difficult times to better days. The article also dwells on the problems of the Argentine economy and the efforts of Isabel Perón, Juan Perón's third wife, who became president upon the death of her husband, to remain in power.

The second article deals with Brazil. It condemns the authoritarian aspects of the present government and the political repression which has stifled opposition voices. Nor does the author have many kind words for the economic growth which has occurred, maintaining that it has failed to benefit the majority of Brazilians. He also asserts that in the last decade Brazil has abandoned its uniqueness and has become an imitator of the Western industrialized countries.

Next, there is a discussion of Venezuela, a country with rich oil reserves and a people who, by and large, have been unaffected by the wealth pouring into the country. Although Venezuela has the highest per capita income in South America, about one third of its people are malnourished, badly housed, and poorly educated. Such facts point to the inability of the government to reach those who most need assistance.

This is followed by a detailed account of the current political and economic scene in Peru, where a military government, without using force, has initiated major social and economic changes throughout the country in order to improve the lot of the people. Agrarian reform has taken place; in some plants, industrial workers now share profits as well as management responsibilities; the educational system is being reorganized to improve quality; the social security system is being revamped. The government faces numerous challenges, not the least of which is that some groups within Peru do not like the reforms at all, and in February 1975 the regime ran into trouble when police officers, demanding higher pay, fought a pitched battle with the army. The regime, whose unpopularity has been growing, promptly suspended all constitutional guarantees.

The extract that follows concerns Uruguay, one of the least known countries in South America. Uruguay is interesting because at one time it had been referred to as a utopia. But it has come upon hard times in the last two decades. The article chronicles the story of the bad luck and bad management which have brought Uruguay to its unhappy state.

The last article in this section deals with Paraguay and its longtime military dictator, General Alberto Stroessner.

ARGENTINA AFTER PERÓN [1]

For three days and nights, the grief-stricken crowd queued for miles in a drenching rain around the National Congress building in Buenos Aires. They waited—tired, hungry and wet—to pay their last respects to Juan Domingo Perón, the man who dominated Argentina's political life for the past twenty-eight years and who died ... [in July

[1] From article in *Newsweek.* 84:34-7. Jl. 15, '74. Copyright Newsweek, Inc. 1974. Reprinted by permission.

1974] at the age of seventy-eight. Some of his countrymen softly sang the Peronist March, "Perón, Perón, how great you are." Some stopped to touch or kiss his body as they filed past the catafalque as he lay in state. And when the coffin, draped in the blue and white flag of Argentina, was borne on an army gun-carriage through the streets to Perón's home in the suburb of Olivos, men and women wept openly and tossed bouquets of white chrysanthemums on the passing cortege. One woman, her face streaked with tears, waved a handkerchief in farewell and asked of no one in particular: "What will become of us now?"

Countless others wondered too, and the reply most often heard was, *"Nada bueno"* ("Nothing good"). Perón's death created a perilous political vacuum in Argentina, and although the country's bitterly warring factions all declared a truce at his passing, it was certain to be brittle and temporary. Argentina's politicians, military leaders and labor officials all found it expedient to pledge their support last week to Perón's successor—his vice president and widow, María Estela Martínez de Perón. And so did the masses. As she rode behind her husband's coffin in the funeral procession, thousands called to her by the name she has adopted: "Isabel, Isabel."

Argentines learned of Perón's death in a broadcast by Mrs. Perón herself. In Buenos Aires, people stood stock still on the sidewalk as her voice came over the radios of parked cars, and throughout the country people sat transfixed before their television screens. "With great pain," she said, her lips trembling, "I must tell the people of the death of a true apostle of peace and nonviolence." She sobbed once, and then in a firm voice added that—in accordance with Argentina's constitution—she had officially assumed the office of the presidency. "I beg of friends and enemies," Mrs. Perón said, "that they lay aside personal passions for the good of a free, just and sovereign fatherland."

Dropout

The question was how long Isabel Perón would choose—or be able—to stay in power as the first woman to serve as leader of a Western Hemisphere country. She could remain in office until 1977, when Perón's term expires, and then, theoretically, she could run to succeed herself. "Who knows?" commented one Argentine last week. "Isabel could turn out to be our Queen Victoria." That seemed most unlikely. A sixth-grade dropout, she met Perón when he was in exile in Panama and she was hoofing with "Joe Herald's Ballet" in the Happyland nightclub. She soon became his private secretary and then his wife. And last year, when Perón returned from foreign exile to run for the presidency, he insisted—to the consternation of many Peronists—that she run for vice president.

Mrs. Perón has conceded that she lacks the qualifications to deal with Argentina's crippling economic and social problems. She also lacks the magnetism of the revered Evita, Perón's second wife, who is still worshiped throughout Argentina. Thus, she enters office with only the barest chance of remaining in it for long. But, given the chaotic conditions in the country, perhaps no one could. "If Perón had lived," said Latin American scholar Milton Barall of Georgetown University, "even he would not have been able to hold on. He died just in time to save the myth."

Confidant

While he lived, Perón never permitted any of his followers to gain enough stature to be considered his heir. But following his death, one Peronist—José López Rega, the right-wing minister of social welfare—appeared to be making a bid for power. A former police corporal and a believer in astrology, López Rega became a close confidant of the late general and is also said to have close ties to Isabel. . . . Although he is the junior cabinet officer, he was the only one besides Mrs. Perón permitted to address the country on national television following Perón's death. The fifty-two-year-old López Rega called on the people to rally around Mrs. Perón, since anything else would be "anti-patriotic, negative and pernicious."

López Rega may be a considerable power behind the throne; his critics call him "Rasputin." But he has no political base—and a number of potent enemies. One well-armed left-wing Peronist group, the Montoneros, which can count on the support of sixty thousand militant supporters, has virtually sworn to assassinate him. The Marxist People's Revolutionary Army, which has a cadre of three thousand terrorists and is the group responsible for a number of kidnappings of Argentine and foreign businessmen, has also vowed to go after López Rega. And military leaders, despite their public professions of support for Mrs. Perón, warned her that their backing was given on one condition: López Rega must go.

Even without behind-the-scenes political intrigue, Mrs. Perón may be driven from office by Argentina's enormous economic and social problems. Inflation has sliced off vast portions of workers' earnings and a new wave of strikes and demonstrations could easily break out soon. Already public confidence in the Argentine economy is eroding; the black market in currency, which is a prime indicator of such confidence, jumped last week to 150 percent of the legal exchange rate. New unrest among workers might easily unseat the new president. "No coalition of government forces that I can conceive," said one political observer in Buenos Aires, "can stand up to a workers' strike."

If disturbances break out, many expect the Peronist movement to revamp Argentina's constitution, name a prime minister to run the country and keep Mrs. Perón on as a figurehead president. In a country as volatile as Argentina, however, it is not out of the question that the military will attempt to take power once again. After years of bumbling government, the generals stood aside for the elections that returned Perón to the presidency last year, and they are apparently not eager to have another try at ruling Argentina. "The military," one US diplomat noted, "is badly burned by the past." But there are many Argentines who fear that a rash of kidnapings, murders and other acts of terror will erupt once the nation finishes mourning Perón's death. . . .

A Man on Horseback

For better or worse, Juan Domingo Perón was one of the mythic figures of twentieth century politics. To his dedicated followers, especially among the *descamisados* (the shirtless ones), the tall, elegant Perón was practically a saint; to his enemies, he was a ruthless demagogue. But whether he was ensconced in the Casa Rosada presidential palace in Buenos Aires or living in luxurious exile in Madrid, Perón was the dominant force in Argentine politics for more than a quarter century. He was "el líder"—a man who accomplished one of the most stunning political comebacks in recent history. Yet, when he died . . . in Buenos Aires after two heart attacks in a period of three hours, Perón—for all the public scrutiny he had received over the years—remained an enigma.

The contradictions that made up Perón were extraordinary. He was a devout Roman Catholic, but his feud with the church helped to bring down his first regime. He was a defender of the oppressed and scourge of the rich, but he surrounded himself with luxury—and when he fled into exile in 1955, he accepted the hospitality of right-wing regimes in Paraguay, the Dominican Republic and Spain. He modeled himself on Franco and Mussolini—and cooperated with Nazi Germany during World War II—but was brought back to office for his second term of power by young Argentines who worshiped Mao Tse-tung and Che Guevara. Perón himself once tried to explain his appeal. "Peronism is mysticism," he said, and true enough, to his followers Perón was often viewed as an infallible, if secular, savior.

Army Coup

The leader of this quasi-religious cult was born October 8, 1895, in Lobos, sixty-five miles south of Buenos Aires. Perón's parents were middle-class—the father of Italian extraction, the mother of mixed Spanish and Indian blood. From the age of fifteen, when he entered military school, his life was the army—and it was the army that catapulted him into politics. As a young colonel, he took part in a coup that put the military in power in 1943, and within three years Perón rose to the top of the heap and became president.

Perón's political strength rested on two pillars—the military and the urban working class. A marriage of nationalism and social reform, Peronism was the forerunner of a political formula that was to reappear throughout the Third World for the next twenty years. Perón himself took care of the nationalism; his second wife, María Eva Duarte, a fiery former actress, carried the message of economic justice to the masses. *"Perón Cumple"* (Perón delivers) said the wall posters, and to a degree he did. He bettered the lot of the Argentine workers, creating a strong trade-union movement and giving them better wages, social security and a sense of dignity. Even today, Juan and "Evita" are remembered in remote villages because the Eva Perón Foundation sent a sewing machine to a cripple or a bicycle to a poor child.

Hysteria

Evita died of cancer in 1952 at the age of thirty-three—and her death traumatized Argentina. Sixteen people died in the crush to view her body, and thousands were treated for hysteria. Argentines prayed to her photograph and some of her followers asked Pope Pius XII to canonize her. As for Perón, he kept her embalmed body in a coffin in his residence.

Perón also bankrupted the nation—morally, politically and economically. Government under the smooth and wily general meant the steady growth of a highly centralized dictatorship. Political opponents were hounded into silence or prison; the courts and universities were purged; newspapers were muzzled or put out of business. Perhaps Perón's most damaging weakness was his monumental inability to understand the simplest economics. In 1955, his fellow military men—egged on by the country's old ruling class and by prelates scandalized by Peronist legislation legalizing prostitution and divorce—moved against Perón. With the army in rebellion and the navy threatening to shell Buenos Aires, Perón yielded and fled into exile aboard a Paraguayan gunboat, vowing all the while to return.

Throughout his long exile, Perón plotted his return to power with Machiavellian cunning. He settled in Madrid, and his villa became a substitute Casa Rosada where he received a continual stream of Argentine politicians who came to suggest deals or receive orders. "I don't know whether I should take the reins of that bucking horse which is Argentina at my age," he would say. But Perón's ambition was rekindled by an ambitious young blonde named María Estela Martínez. An ex-professional dancer who preferred to be called Isabel, she married Perón secretly in 1961. Devoted to the Evita cult, she took personal charge of her heroine's corpse and, more important, convinced the aging but all-too-willing Perón that it was his mission to return to lead Argentina.

Reinstated

As one regime after another floundered, Perón's time eventually came again. In 1973, the discredited military government called elections that the Peronists won. In short order, Perón's stand-in stepped down, new elections were called and Perón was elected with 62 percent of the vote. Eighteen years after he had fled, Perón was reinstated in the Casa Rosada.

"I am the only element holding the Peronist party together," he observed accurately. But because of his fragile health, in his final year he was hardly more than a spiritual symbol. Argentina continued to be plagued by political terrorism and a catalog of social and economic travails.

On his death, even his political enemies acknowledged that Perón was one of the most remarkable figures in Argentine history. But his legacy was grievously flawed. He lent a certain grandeur and instilled a sense of worth in thousands of his *descamisados*. And yet Juan Perón left behind a confused, divided and violent land.

BRAZIL: THE IMITATIVE SOCIETY [2]

One hundred fifty years ago, Brazil broke its political ties with Portugal. While serving as regent of Brazil, Prince Pedro, the young Braganza heir to the Portuguese throne, unilaterally declared Brazil's independence. With most of the Western Hemisphere independent of Europe by 1822, Pedro had little choice. He could declare Brazil's independence and become its emperor, or he could stand by while the restive Brazilian elite declared their own independence and established a new government without the guiding hand of the Braganzas. The former course was obviously his preference, and the Braganzas ruled until the republic was established in 1889. Although nominally independent, Brazil changed little throughout most of the nineteenth century. True, a small Brazilian elite exercised political power in place of the Portuguese, but institutions, customs and social patterns remained much as they had been in the colonial past. Great Britain dominated the economic life of the new nation at least as much as Portugal had during the colonial period.

Fifty years ago, a group of writers, poets and artists, weary of Brazil's slavish imitation of European culture, gathered at the Municipal Theatre in São Paulo to proclaim their country's intellectual independence. During the

[2] From article by E. Bradford Burns, professor of Latin American history at the University of California at Los Angeles. *Nation*. 215:17-20. Jl. 10, '72. Reprinted by permission.

"Modern Art Week" of 1922, they pleaded with their compatriots to forget the marble temples and Gothic churches of Europe and contemplate the lush vegetation and natural wealth of Brazil. They turned the eyes of the nation inward, an introspection which produced a series of fascinating studies of the Brazilian character and soul. A new type of writer—of whom Gilberto Freyre and Jorge Amado are best known in the US—created a style, language and subject matter that were uniquely Brazilian.

Having achieved their new intellectual insight, the Brazilians became increasingly aware of their economic dependency. If Great Britain had dominated the economy in the nineteenth century, the US did so after World War I. The great financial debacle in Western Europe and the US in 1929 adversely affected Brazil and prompted the new government of Getúlio Vargas, the man who, alive or dead, shaped Brazil in the 1930-64 period, to take measures to reduce Brazil's economic dependency. He increased governmental planning and participation in the economy. A steel company was founded in the 1940s; a national oil monopoly, Petrobrás, was authorized in 1953; a company to encourage and control the production of electrical energy, Electrobrás, came into being in 1962, the same year in which the government promulgated a law to limit profit remissions abroad.

Those measures, taken to increase Brazil's political, intellectual and economic independence, were dramatically reversed after April 1, 1964. On that day the military swept into power, deposing the constitutionally selected president, João Goulart, and ending nineteen years of successful experimentation with democracy. Vocal and powerful elements of the upper and middle classes, fearing the populist tendencies of the Goulart government, had called upon the military to put an end to further reform. The officers had intervened in politics before but customarily withdrew after a short time, leaving the government in civilian hands. Not so in 1964. The officers resolved to exercise power themselves and they have done so with increasing harshness ever since.

One of the most surprising results of these ... years of military rule has been the surrender of much of Brazil's independence of action and choice, so painfully won during the preceding decades. The originality characteristic of Brazilian political and intellectual life during the 1950s and early 1960s has disappeared, smothered by an official disapproval of trends prevalent in that period and denounced by an insecure middle class that is eager to imitate as superior whatever originates abroad.

With Brazil now exercising less independence of action than at any time in memory, it is ironic that in 1972 the nation lavishly ... [commemorated] 150 years of political independence. The irony has not gone unnoticed. What happened to a slogan posted on a wall in downtown Rio de Janeiro indicates that at least some Brazilians are aware of the absurdity of the commemorations: a vertical line drawn in the appropriate place in *"Viva Independência"* (Long live independence) transformed the meaning to *"Viva In/dependência"* (Live in dependency).

Nearly every aspect of Brazilian life feels the weight of the new dependency. In no realm is it more obvious or heavier than in foreign policy. Hardly had the military settled into office in 1964 than the officers denounced and reversed the independent foreign policy which the previous three governments had tried to implement. Contemptuous of those attempts to gain leadership for Brazil in the Third World, the generals decried the threat of international communism and pledged to follow Washington in the struggle against the East, unmindful apparently that a previously bipolar world was rapidly becoming multipolar. Accordingly, and in contrast to previous action, Brazil broke diplomatic relations with Cuba, opposed throughout the last half of the 1960s the seating of the People's Republic of China in the United Nations, supported Portugal's African policies, and expressed solidarity with the US in Vietnam.

Contravening a century-old policy of nonintervention, Brazilian soldiers marched side by side with the US Marines into the Dominican Republic to prevent the legitimate and reformist government of Juan Bosch from returning to power. A psychotic fear of communism, not at all uncommon among the Latin American elite, propels Brazil's foreign policy and prompts an intimate union with Washington. All of its foreign ministers since 1964 have also served as ambassadors to the US. A frank minister of foreign relations in the mid-1960s startled even the subservient Brazilian press with his declaration, "What's good for the US is good for Brazil."

The political liberty that once nourished the careers of a host of original and effective leaders is now a distant memory. After April 1, 1964, liberty died a quick death and with it any independent political thought. The generals abolished freedom of speech, press and assembly; packed the supreme court to guarantee its acquiescence; disbanded the lively array of political parties to create two lifeless "official" parties (the difference between them, as one wag noted, is that while one answers "Yes, sir," to the government, the other simply responds "Yes"); forbade any free or direct elections; abrogated the rights of thousands of Brazilians, including 3 former presidents, 5 senators, and 88 deputies; filled the jails with political prisoners, hundreds of whom have been tortured, some unto death. Since 1964, there have been more than 35,000 political arrests; at least 10,000 political prisoners languish in Brazilian jails today; 2,000 Brazilians live in political exile.

Political repression continues. In ... [1972] the military police swept through Rio de Janeiro, arresting more than 200 students whom they branded as subversives because they had the temerity to ask for more schools. The youth correctly pointed out that the dictatorship was spending more money on military hardware than on the nation's education. Since Brazil is not fighting any foreign wars, or likely to fight any in the foreseeable future, it is obvious that the hardware has been bought to repress the people. The increasing brutality of the military dictatorship has dampened, at least temporarily, the customary good humor of the Brazilians.

In fact, the average Brazilian has little to be good-humored about. Although news reports constantly remind the world of Brazil's economic "miracle"—a recent economic growth of 9 to 10 percent a year—they neglect to mention that the "miracle" has failed to benefit the vast majority of the Brazilians. Wages lag behind prices. In 1965, the wage earner lost 14 percent of his purchasing power; in 1966, he lost another 22 percent. In 1968, [the] minister of labor . . . conservatively estimated that the workers' real wages had fallen between 15 and 30 percent in the previous four years; in 1971 an increase of the minimum wage still fell 5 percent short of the rise in the cost of living for the preceding year. In 1972 President Emílio Garrastazú Médici conceded, "The economy is going well, the people not so well." Calling that an understatement, Oscar Pedroso Horta, leader of the otherwise docile Brazilian Democratic Movement, one of the two toothless "official" political parties, claimed . . . that "housewives were battling to make ends meet, while their money was losing 20 percent to 25 percent a year because of inflation." The poorest 80 percent of the Brazilians saw their share of the GNP drop from 35 to 27.5 percent during the decade of the 1960s.

On the other hand, there can be no doubt that the industrial elite and the upper urban middle class have profited handsomely in the last eight years of military dictatorship. The richest 5 percent of the population increased their share of the GNP from 44 percent to 50 percent during the 1960s.

Foreign investors have also fared well. Liberal tax incentives, the stability and order which a dictatorship can guarantee, an immunity from strikes, and a generally benign attitude toward foreign businessmen have attracted and kept more than $4 billion of direct investment in

Brazil, almost half of which comes from the US. With a generous hand, the military rulers have distributed mining concessions to foreigners. They sold the only Brazilian automobile and truck company, Fábrica Nacional de Motores, to Alfa Romeo, rewrote the profits remittance law promulgated by the previous government over the protests of the foreign business community, weakened the once sacrosanct Petrobrás by awarding contracts to more and more foreign companies to prospect and drill for oil, and opened the petrochemical industries to foreign investment.

Denationalization of Brazilian industry has been accelerating. As early as December 16, 1966, *Time* reported that foreign investors had gained control of 50 percent of Brazilian industry since the 1964 military coup. By 1968, ... [a] Uruguayan journalist ... gave a far gloomier report: foreign capital controlled 40 percent of the capital market, 62 percent of the foreign trade, 82 percent of the maritime transport, 77 percent of the overseas airlines, 100 percent of the motor vehicle production, 100 percent of the tire production, more than 80 percent of the pharmaceutical industry, nearly 50 percent of the chemical industry, 59 percent of machine production, 47 percent of aluminum, and 90 percent of cement.

In its drive to attract foreign capital, the military government also seems quite willing to overlook the antipollution standards it once decreed. In early 1972, [the] minister of planning ... revealed that antipollution standards would be reduced to permit foreign investors to proceed with the building of wood-pulp paper plants on the central coast. The cost of cleaning up the environment, if it is ever done, will doubtless be borne by the patient Brazilians.

It has become customary for top governmental officials to move from their posts of command and influence in Brasília [the capital] to lucrative jobs in the Brazilian branches of foreign companies. ... Little wonder then that the foreign companies enjoy direct access to inner governmental councils.

In August 1971, when the editor-publisher Hélio Fernandes had the courage to accuse the military on the front page of his *Tribuna da Imprensa* of supporting an unpopular government instead of taking the lead to free Brazil from foreign economic domination, he was arrested and his paper closed down for forty-eight hours. The military does not look kindly on expressions of economic nationalism, and promptly silences anyone who might criticize foreign investments. But censorship goes far beyond this: it reaches every media, from newspapers to song lyrics, to eradicate even the most veiled criticism of the regime. Such rigorous censorship results in a bizarre, really surrealistic press. Most of what is printed is pap. "President Opens Grape Festival," yawned the headlines one morning.... On another day in the same week, Brazilians must have stared in disbelief at this headline: "Brazil Is Irretrievably Antitotalitarian, Says Minister of War."

Often the censor forbids the publication of important news. For example, there was no news of the coup d'état of December 13, 1968, when the military measurably increased its hold on the country. Prohibited from publishing that news, the papers contained a weird assortment of miscellaneous information which demonstrated that not all Brazilians had lost their sense of humor. The staid *Correio da Manha* of Rio de Janeiro bore the glaring headline, "Rich Cat Dies of Heart Attack in Chicago." The *Jornal do Brasil* carried prominently a wry weather report, "Weather black. Temperature suffocating. The air is unbreathable. The country is being swept by a strong wind." The control of information reached a ludicrous climax in November 1971, when President Médici issued a decree authorizing himself to make secret decrees—which is to say, laws that are not divulged to the public. One wonders how it can be possible to obey a law that is secret.

Rigorous censorship produces intellectual sterility. The military dictatorship has managed to stunt all academic and artistic growth, and that, in turn, has enabled foreign culture to dominate. The intellectual independence so proudly and ably asserted in 1922 is no longer visible.

The shelves of leading bookstores are bare of any exciting new titles. Intellectuals can no longer debate new ideas in print or suggest alternative programs. In any case, few Brazilians can afford to buy books today. The military government removed the subsidy on paper with the result that the price of books has skyrocketed. They are a luxury now, within the reach only of a bourgeoisie whose tastes favor French, English and American authors.

Only a decade ago Brazilian music commanded an international audience. The sound of the *bossa nova* was heard throughout Europe and the United States. Musicians such as João Gilberto, Antônio Carlos Jobim, Sérgio Mendes and Edú Lôbo were as popular abroad as at home. "The Girl from Ipanema" became a hit song in the United States, and the younger set greeted "The Band" with enthusiasm. But when the musicians put protest to music, the military censors became instant music critics. One of the most popular songs in the late 1960s was called "Walking," whose lyrics could be construed as mild protest against the unpopular military dictatorship. . . .

"Subversive," charged the general in charge of public security in Rio de Janeiro, and he cautioned that the song has "a musical cadence of the Mao Tse-tung type that can easily serve as the anthem for student street demonstrations." The police began to harass composers and singers, many of whom fled into exile. Censorship of music went from the ridiculous to the absurd. Recently the composition of one of Brazil's most gifted and popular composers . . . was banned because the lyrics claimed, "Tomorrow will be another day." The result has been to discourage the original music for which Brazil was gaining international recognition. Thus far into the 1970s music faithfully echoes foreign trends.

The theatre is in the same situation. Censorship has silenced some of the best dramatists and ended the so-

called "popular" theatre. Here too, with subsidies gone or
sharply reduced, few can afford the box-office prices. Foreign
influence dominates the Brazilian stage. The most popular
show in Rio de Janeiro during the first months of 1972
was called, in English not in Portuguese, *Brazil Export
Show '72* and starred the Jo-Jo Smith dancers with choreog-
raphy by Lenny Bruce. The expensive and elegant show
looked like a flawed copy of a second-rate TV musical. The
producers ignored the lively and original Brazilian music
and dance to give the audience what they must have considered to be a chic Broadway revue. The upper-middle-
class audience clapped its approval.

Imitation pervades Brazilian society to the point that
the aping of foreign styles is both embarrassing and sad.
With the temperature hovering in the mid-90s in February
and March and with a humidity to match, middle-class
matrons of Rio de Janeiro paraded about in pants suits.
They dress their children the same way, and one feels for
them as they trudge along the street in their knee boots
(still in summer). Here the poor have at least the advantage
that they must make do with sandals. One must suffer to
be fashionable—particularly when one imports his ideas of
fashion from distant and much cooler cities.

Not surprisingly those same middle-class imitators are
abandoning their Brazilian cuisine for hot dogs, French
fries and Coca-Cola. The *bahianas*, those marvelous cooks
of distinctive Afro-Brazilian delicacies, have practically disappeared from the street corners of the major cities, where
for centuries they sold their food. In their place, neon-lit,
chrome-countered eateries have sprung up everywhere. Bear-
ing the names of Bob's, Kidd's, Rick's, and Gordon's, these
meccas of the middle class offer the same quick snack a
teenager would relish in Kansas City or Denver.

Imitation of foreign models in no way embarrasses the
middle class. To the contrary, they plaster their automobile
windows with decals reading, "Brazil, Love It or Leave It."

And when they say "it," they mean their imitative Brazil, devoid of the sin of originality or native genius.

Quite understandably, foreign governments smile on the new subservience of a Brazil that once challenged their investors and threatened to pursue a course of political, diplomatic, intellectual and economic independence. None has supported the Brazilian military more enthusiastically than the US. President Johnson made no effort to disguise his pleasure over the military coup d'état on April 1, 1964. He telegraphed congratulations to the officers within hours after they had seized power (even before a cabinet had been formed) and expressed his admiration for the way the Brazilians had settled the matter "within the framework of constitutional democracy and without civil strife." In a bit of political baroque, US Ambassador Lincoln Gordon classified the military takeover as "the single most decisive victory for freedom in the mid-twentieth century." US aid in excess of $1.6 billion cascaded upon the new government. Washington has supplied more military aid to Brazil than to any other country in this hemisphere, aid which has no apparent use other than for "internal security."

The "land of the free" has helped to train the police force of a country in which there are at least 10,000 political prisoners, not even the façade of freedom, and no popular support for the government. . . . It is believed that during the . . . [1960s] the public safety program assisted in training more than 100,000 policemen in Brazil; and an additional 523 were brought to the US to learn more specialized skills, including riot control and counterinsurgency. . . .

A litany of dreary social and economic statistics shows that the military government has done little, if anything, to solve the basic problems of the nation's 100 million inhabitants: fully 50 percent of the population is illiterate; out of every 100 heads of family, 70 do not earn even the minimum wage equivalent to $35 a month; more than three quarters of the farmers have no land of their own; 1.6 percent of the landowners own nearly 50 percent of the land;

in the huge Northeast, the life expectancy barely reaches 30 years, a child dies every 42 seconds, 85 per hour, 2,040 a day. In short, Brazil is a land where poverty, hunger, unemployment, underemployment, social waste, illiteracy and chronic sickness abound.

Atop a high hill dominating the quiet waters of Botafogo Bay in Rio de Janeiro stands a giant Coca-Cola sign. Blinking rhythmically in the evening air, it casts its bright reflection across the waters to taunt the Brazilians, reminding them that so much of their present culture is being imported, that so much of their genius is being suppressed, that so much of their originality is being discarded.

VENEZUELA GROWS FAST, BUT MANY STAY POOR [3]

The view of Caracas from the slum dwellings that infest the surrounding green hills and ravines is one of movement, growth and hope.

"Our country is rich but our people are poor, and this must change," says Carlos Andrés Pérez, who was elected in . . . [1973] to a five-year term as president. Essentially, his program is to improve the distribution of wealth and obtain more benefits from the country's principal resource, oil.

Venezuela, fifth among exporters and one of the chief suppliers to the United States, has joined the others in exacting higher taxes and royalties by raising the posted, or tax-reference, price per barrel. The action was the first outside the Arab bloc.

Caracas was virtually built on oil and its fortunes have accompanied those of oil. A bucolic colonial city of barely 100,000 half a century ago, before the oil boom, it has 2.7 million people, or a fourth of the country's population, today.

[3] From article by Marvine Howe, staff correspondent, South America. New York *Times*. p 2. Ja. 3, '74. © 1974 by the New York Times Company. Reprinted by permission.

There has been considerable waste, injustice and ostentation in the spending of the oil revenues. Nevertheless, Caracas is a monument of prosperity in Latin America, with a maze of superhighways and monstrous traffic snarls, skyscrapers and vast housing developments, elegant suburbs, shopping centers and country clubs, an army of construction cranes and, above all, opportunity.

A Colombian chemical engineer who was earning about $250 a month at home came here recently and is getting four or five times that.

A Child With Dreams

A child of the slums—they are known as *ranchos*—is thirteen-year-old Ernesto Zamora, who dreams of becoming an architect, and perhaps he will. Now he goes to a public school. His widowed mother works as a maid to support nine children.

The Zamoras live in Hornos de Cal—(the Lime Kiln), a brick and concrete slum overlooking the luxurious Caracas Hilton. The kilns are being razed, the population will be moved and the Zamoras hope to get a new low-cost, high-rise apartment just down the hill.

Roughly a million people live in *ranchos* in greater Caracas. Governments have razed them time and again and have poured money into housing projects, but there are always new slums, and the problem seems to get worse.

The trouble is one of the highest rates of urbanization in the world, along with an annual population increase of 3.5 percent, one of the highest rates in the world and the highest in Latin America (Costa Rica equals it).

The oil rush, or rather the rush to the cities, got under way shortly after World War II. Money went into public works projects, mainly highways. The roads, intended to open up the interior, had the reverse effect, making it easier for the rural population to move to the city.

Social Development Lags

Social development has simply not kept pace with the population increase. In 1936 less than 30 percent of the population lived in places with 2,500 inhabitants; today about 77 percent are urban.

Geographically, Venezuela resembles a bird with giant wings ready to take off. About the size of Texas and Oklahoma combined, the country is divided into four distinct regions: a tropical coastal zone bordering the Caribbean Sea, a cooler northern coastal range and the Andes in the west, the hot llanos plains and, to the south, the Guayana highlands and the Amazon jungles.

Venezuela is the closest South American country to the US, geographically and in many other ways. Originally sparsely settled, she has become a pole of attraction. About 60 percent of the population is mestizo—of mixed white, black and Indian ancestry. An important influx after World War II brought people from Spain, Portugal and Italy, and there is a German colony. Now there is a steady flow of Colombians seeking higher wages; it is said that there are half a million here illegally.

The once-rigid social system, dominated by a small group of landholders, merchants, politicians and military men, has given way to a fluid cosmopolitan society with economic and political power increasingly in the hands of the middle class—intellectuals, bureaucrats, small entrepreneurs, managers, technicians, white-collar workers and skilled industrial workers.

The middle class is consumer-oriented, with tastes similar to those in the US. Venezuelans like big American cars and drive-ins, soda fountains and pizzerias, credit cards and baseball, and private schools for their children. They work hard and visit a psychologist when things go wrong.

Even the *rancho* people in Caracas consider themselves middle class, and by Latin American standards they are. Most have electricity and running water, radios or television sets and refrigerators, and many can boast of a brother or a son who is a doctor or a lawyer.

Basically there are two Venezuelas: Caracas and a few rapidly developing northern cities, and the rest of the country, with declining villages struggling for a subsistence existence.

Places like Caucagua, only about fifty miles from Caracas, are another world. The population, under 5,000, is mostly black. People sit in the shade of banana trees in front of mud and stick houses and talk about Caracas. Barefoot children with ballooning stomachs play in the dusty streets. There is a church, a shady village square, a cafe blaring Caribbean music and not much else.

Things are worse in the central plains state of Apure, where the farmers and cattle raisers live much as they did two centuries ago. The only difference is that people can move about by plane; there are still almost no roads.

Virtually Untouched Area

The vast southern Amazon territory, with a population of only 23,000, has been virtually untouched. The Indians there live as they did in pre-Columbian times. The government development program known as the Conquest of the South began only in 1969.

In sum, it is said, about a third of the population is poorly fed, poorly housed, poorly clothed and poorly schooled. Yet Venezuela has the highest per capita income in Latin America—$1,200—and foreign-exchange reserves of $1.7 billion, among the largest on a per capita basis.

It is a lopsided economy, with the oil industry providing two thirds of government revenue and 90 percent of export earnings, but employing only about 16,000 people.

In view of the favorable statistics, the US aid mission can no longer justify a program of technical training and urban-development assistance and is closing shop.

The presidential election of December 9 [1973] was a triumph for the young Venezuelan democracy, which only dates from 1958, when a popular rising ousted the dictator Marcos Pérez Jiménez.

President-elect Pérez, a Social Democrat, said in his initial declarations that he wanted to come to terms with the US, "our first market," but made it clear that he would drive a hard bargain.

"We will accept foreign cooperation to develop our oil reserves, but on our conditions" he said in a recent interview, giving an insight into the aggressive oil policy he has in mind.

Mr. Pérez's chief problems are internal: the urbanization, inflation, stagnant agriculture, unemployment and wide disparities in income.

Although previous governments have poured funds into public works and expanded official payrolls, unemployment remains acute; economists estimate that a quarter of the population is jobless. To make matters worse, Venezuela really joined the worldwide inflationary movement in 1973. Officially, prices rose 9 percent; unofficial estimates put the figure near 20 percent.

For a decade prices have been stable because of fixed, subsidized food prices. Agricultural production was chronically poor, but it did not matter because it was easier and cheaper to import food from Colombia and the US. Now, however, with world commodity prices soaring, the government has had to relax price controls.

One of Mr. Pérez's main themes in the campaign against eleven other candidates was the urgent need to modernize and develop agriculture, "the motor of our economy."

There has been much talk of the Orinoco tar belt, which is said to have the largest known reserves in the Western Hemisphere. These deposits, discovered three decades ago, are high in sulphur content and would require huge capital and technological investment. The US has shown interest in the Orinoco field.

Concerned over the vanishing oil, governments have sought alternative sources of wealth.

On the southern bank of the Orinoco there is a new city Ciudad Guayana, which will be the capital for heavy industry. Some $1.4 billion has been spent on a metallurgical complex, mining and hydro-electric power.

The other major development is El Tablazo, a petrochemical complex at the entrance of Lake Maracaibo, where most of the productive oil fields are found.

PERU'S AMBIGUOUS REVOLUTION [4]

Headed by General Juan Velasco Alvarado, Peru's "Revolutionary Government of the Armed Forces" has now completed more than five years in power. [Cuban Premier] Fidel Castro has acclaimed the Peruvian undertaking; [the late Argentine President] Juan Perón has extolled it. *Peruanista* factions have emerged in the armed forces of several South American countries.

The Peruvian regime is generally seen not as the typical Latin American *caudillo* [i.e., military] government but rather as an essentially institutional effort. Although a government of force, it is widely regarded as relatively unrepressive. More important, although the nation's force for order, the military has set out to transform many basic areas of national life. Major structural reforms have affected land tenure and water rights, labor-management relations, the educational system, the state's role in the economy and in the communications media, the role of foreign enterprise in Peru's economy, and even fundamental concepts of economic and political relationships. Particularly noteworthy has been the regime's announced determination to move steadily away from capitalist principles by creating a new "social property" economic sector (based on collective ownership of the means of production), destined to become the "predominant" mode of economic organization. And the

[4] From article by Abraham F. Lowenthal, author and scholar on Latin American affairs. *Foreign Affairs*. 52:799-817. Jl. '74. Reprinted by permission from *Foreign Affairs*, July 1974. Copyright 1974 by Council on Foreign Relations, Inc.

regime has emphasized its aim to promote a drastic change in national values, to create a "new Peruvian man," one dedicated to "solidarity, not individualism."

From various foreign perspectives, Peru's current process of military-directed change is regarded with hope. For many on the international Left, Peru's approach seems especially significant, particularly now that the "Chilean way" has been so abruptly closed. [See Section IV, "Chile in Turmoil," below.] From this vantage point, Peru is contrasted with Brazil. Leftist intellectuals have lost their jobs and rights and some have suffered torture in Brazil; many of their counterparts in Peru are advising the regime or are at least sympathetic to it. Bishops in Brazil condemn their regime; Peruvian bishops generally support theirs. The Brazilian regime promotes capitalist expansion, national and foreign, while the Peruvian government announces its aim to move away from capitalism. And while Brazil ties itself ever more closely to the US, Peru has acted to reduce its dependence on Washington.

Paradoxically, many international lenders and even some investors also regard Peru's experiment favorably. The military regime has earned plaudits for its prudent fiscal management and for its pragmatism in dealing with foreign companies. From this standpoint, Peru's regime is contrasted with Castro's and with Chile's under [the late President] Allende. Whatever the short-term nuisance of renegotiating contracts and absorbing nationalist verbal attacks, at least foreign investors think the military regime is making Peru safe for them, now and for some time to come.

Within Peru, the military regime's program is not so widely acclaimed. Articulate observers from both sides of the political spectrum assail the government. Though the traditional (Moscow-line) Communist party openly supports the military regime, many on the Left regard it as far from "revolutionary," but rather as an ally of international capitalism, exploiting the Peruvian masses for the sake of dominant minorities. From the Right, the military government's program is also viewed with deepening distrust. Even those businessmen who had successfully adjusted themselves to countless changes they might have resisted under other circumstances found themselves alarmed in 1973 by the sudden nationalization of the entire fishmeal industry (Peru's main foreign-exchange earner) and by the repeated, escalating stress on "social property."

Despite its international stature, the Peruvian regime finds itself almost bereft of conspicuous support at home. No group is likely soon to displace or even seriously challenge the military, but the government encounters concerted opposition within many important sectors: labor, business, peasants, students, and professionals; one election after another reflects antiregime sentiment. Some backing, particularly among the urban poor and among highland peasants who have benefited already from the agrarian reform, is demonstrated from time to time, but contrary indications are more apparent. General strikes in several provincial areas forced the regime to suspend constitutional guarantees temporarily in mid-1973 and again later that year. The National System to Support Social Mobilization (SINAMOS), established in 1971 partly to organize support for the government, has instead been the object of intensifying attack from all sides, even from within the regime. And middle-class distress is especially perceptible. Housewives, bureaucrats, teachers, taxi drivers, secretaries: all are grumbling.

How should the Peruvian process be characterized? What accounts for its international reputation, and for its trouble at home? What has the Peruvian military regime accomplished? Where is the regime heading, or likely to head?

Economic and Political Changes

The current Peruvian process cannot yet be easily labeled. Many of the regime's key activities remain ambiguous or apparently contradictory. In other areas, gaps have developed between rhetoric and practice and it is hard to tell which, if either, will eventually be modified.

In the economic sphere, the regime's most obvious accomplishment has been to expand and fortify what used to be one of South America's weakest states. The government has announced its intent to control all industries it defines as "basic." It has already taken over, in addition to the fishmeal industry, a major share of mining and metal refining; all petroleum refining, most petroleum marketing, and some oil exploration; the railroad, telephone, telex, and cable companies, and Peru's international air carrier; cement companies; a steadily increasing share of electric utilities; 51 percent of every television station and at least 25 percent of each radio station; cotton, sugar, and mineral exporting; importing and distributing of several key commodities; considerable food marketing; a majority of the banking system and of the insurance business; all reinsurance; and even the operation of the airport's duty free store and of a small chinchilla farm. Incipient government activity in pharmaceutical manufacturing and distribution may portend further expansion in this and other areas. All told, the state's share of national investment has jumped to almost half, compared with 13 percent in 1965 (though this change reflects some decline in private capital formation as well as the expansion of government spending).

The Peruvian state's increasing strength has been evident in many other ways as well. All sorts of previously flouted regulations are now being taken more seriously, as Peruvians experience, in some ways for the first time, a government that governs. Strict regulation of credit, the use of foreign exchange and other major aspects of national economic life is increasingly a fact; collection of taxes long on the books has risen substantially. The public sector's capacity is strengthening as professionals from business and the universities take government jobs.

But while the Peruvian state grows, the military regime repeatedly asserts it does not mean to end major private economic activity. When the fishmeal nationalization shocked the private sector (the official 1971-1975 national plan had assured that the fishmeal industry would remain private), no less than seven cabinet ministers each stressed within a week that the measure was exceptional and that complete abandonment of private enterprise was by no means contemplated. Reassurances to private business have not been limited to verbal expressions; generous tax incentives, tariff breaks, efforts to recognize Lima's stock exchange and other measures to stimulate private investment and reinvestment have accompanied the moves in some sectors toward state ownership. Repeated government statements advocate "economic pluralism" and talk of four types of enterprise (state, "social property," reformed private, and unreformed private for small-scale firms). No one explains convincingly, however, how such very different modes of economic organization can effectively coexist. Not only Peruvian businessmen, but even the regime's own former minister of economy and finance, have had to call for clarification of the "rules of the game" under which Peru's economy is to operate.

In the political arena, the military regime has been similarly active, but again with ambiguous results. The government has vowed to destroy the traditional political system dominated by special interests and to replace it with one open equally to the influence of all citizens, a "social democracy of full participation." Five years have sufficed to show that the task of destruction is being rapidly accomplished, but the second task is still far from realization.

The military regime has systematically undercut almost all organizations politically influential in Peru before 1968, except the church and, of course, the armed forces. Established parties have been severely hampered. Economic interest groups have been crippled; the once-powerful National Agrarian Society has been dissolved, and the National Industries Society has been stripped of its formal standing, legally forbidden to represent itself as "national," and has had its president deported. The government has weakened the labor unions by playing rivals off against each other, and there are signs it expects to move eventually toward a gov-

ernment-sponsored and controlled united labor confederation. Lima's newspapers, once influential, have been largely
cowed into utter blandness. The judicial system, perceived
by the regime as a restraint, has been "reorganized" and is
being made much more responsive to government desires.
Private universities, until 1969 governed individually, have
had their autonomy curtailed by the creation of a central
university system. Autonomous peasant federations, which
gained some strength in the 1960s, were first pushed toward
atrophy and then effectively banned under a law establishing
a National Agrarian Confederation. Individuals and families
who only five years ago were among Peru's most powerful—
Pedro Beltrán, the Prados, the Pardos, the Gildemeisters,
and the Ayulos, to name just a few—have had their influence, if not their wealth, very sharply reduced.

What is not clear, however, is whether the new political
order is really to be anything different from a particularly
efficient version of a traditional dictatorship, governed this
time by a military-technocrat coalition. Despite all the regime's talk about full participation, very few Peruvians have
a prescribed role in influencing government decisions, and
few feel that the regime is responsive to their claims. It is no
wonder that the regime lacks public support; citizens, particularly those whose views used to find expression through
established political channels, resent an autocratic regime,
completely military at the Cabinet level, which can act
arbitrarily without restraint.

The government's dealings with labor and peasant unions, professional and student organizations, business lob-
bies and other groups suggest that the regime distrusts any
autonomous organizations, and wishes to deal only with
units established or legitimized by the regime. The implicit
—and sometimes explicit—concept for political organization
is corporatist. The regime is steadily building up the apparatus by which one group after another is to be tied directly to the executive, which will attempt to harmonize all
interests perceived by the regime as legitimate and expressed

through channels considered appropriate. Political parties are not so regarded; persons with recent party responsibilities are specifically prohibited from becoming officials of various of the newly created participatory mechanisms, e.g., in the shantytowns, in educational units, in agricultural cooperatives, etc. Although repeatedly proclaiming its desire for participation and dialogue, the government evinces increasing impatience with those who question any of a number of central ideas. In short, the regime is authoritarian, and increasingly so.

Stable government without severe repression does set Peru apart from its immediate neighbors. (Brazil's regime is impressively stable but surely repressive, Chile's under Allende was repressive but unstable, while Chile's current junta is so brutally repressive as probably ultimately to be unstable, Ecuador's government is neither stable nor repressive, and Bolivia currently suffers a regime that is both unstable and repressive.) Yet a closer look at contemporary Peru provides a somewhat murkier view. Protesting miners and peasants have been gunned down on occasion, as so often before in Peru's history. The press has been muzzled. Leading antiregime personalities have been harassed and over a score have been deported. The regime has repeatedly shown that it prefers to quiet opposition by accommodation rather than by force. But when push comes to shove, the regime acts without regard for the niceties of constitutional doctrine. Several jailings and deportations within the past year, and some blatant instances of censorship, suggest that the limits within which free discussion is permitted in Peru may be narrowing as time goes on and problems mount.

When all is said and done, however, one cannot dismiss the Peruvian military's talk of "full participation" as mere rhetoric. The regime's spokesmen may well be right in asserting that only harsh treatment of the previous power structure could facilitate the eventual expression of mass participation. Now that the preliminary job is mostly done, some efforts have been initiated, especially through

SINAMOS and through the educational and industrial community mechanisms, to decentralize decision making and transfer it to the local level. At least a few of the top government leaders, especially in SINAMOS, and many of its operating personnel, seem sincerely committed to helping peasants, shantytown dwellers, parents of schoolchildren, and industrial workers organize to achieve effective power. While much of the regime's activity seems aimed (successfully so) at demobilizing previously influential Peruvian groups, SINAMOS appears to be politicizing and "raising consciousness" among several sectors which will eventually be in a position to pressure the army itself. It would appear that the regime is taking at least some first steps to redeem its promise to provide for new forms of participation, even by those mostly unrepresented in Peru. Whether these steps will eventually influence the regime's course substantially, or whether they will signify but a minor or temporary countercurrent, remains to be seen.

In foreign policy, the Peruvian regime is widely acknowledged to be inventive and imaginative. Not only have diplomatic relations been established with the Soviet Union, China and Cuba, but each of these ties has opened up significant possibilities for trade diversification and eventual expansion. The USSR bought over 15 percent of Peru's sugar exports in 1973, China bought over 10 percent of Peru's copper, and both Cuba and China were important purchasers of Peru's fishmeal in 1972 (when Peru last had extra fishmeal to sell and badly needed a market). Substantial Eastern European investment and technical cooperation have been obtained. Major Japanese loans and investment have begun to come in, both for infrastructure and for industrial facilities.

All these steps, together with Peru's role in . . . international organizations and its spirited championing of the 200-mile territorial limit, have been portrayed as reducing Peru's "dependence," principally on the US. Government spokesmen repeatedly claim . . . that Peru has now regained its dignity. And they suggest that important economic decisions affecting Peru, once taken in New York and Washington, are now taken in Lima.

The major growth sectors of the Peruvian economy—petroleum and mining—are still mostly premised on major foreign private investment, however. The military regime has signed no less than seventeen contracts with foreign oil companies, and though their terms are probably more satisfactory to Peru than previous contracts, they appear to be at least as generous to the foreign firms as comparable arrangements in other countries, such as Indonesia, not noted for their revolutionary credentials. In the industrial area, even Brazil's avowedly proforeign investment regime gets better terms, at least in some sectors, than Peru can command. It is hard to say, therefore, whether Peru's new foreign policy amounts to much more than a particularly flamboyant adjustment to the shifting realities of international power and to new fashions in international rhetoric. Making that adjustment intelligently is no negligible accomplishment, but it is not so fundamental a change as Peru's spokesmen herald.

The Peruvian military stakes its revolutionary claim primarily on the structural reforms it has designed, promulgated, and begun to administer. Here, again, no easy label is appropriate.

The agrarian reform of 1969 has brought a substantial redistribution of land in a country where its degree of concentration had long been exceptionally high. Within less than five years, the regime has taken over virtually all Peru's large estates, beginning with the vast sugar plantations (which were not to be affected at all under the previous Peruvian agrarian reform legislation) and moving next to the highland areas. Land has been expropriated and title redistributed at a pace faster than that of any recent Latin American reform but Cuba's, and perhaps Chile's under Allende. Legislation affecting access to water, without which land ownership may be useless, has also been sharply revised.

The industrial or enterprise reform provides workers a share not only in profits but also in management. Workers within each firm employing six or more workers receive a fixed percentage of their company's profits, some distributed immediately in cash but more retained as commonly owned shares in the firm, which is eventually to be half-owned by the "labor community," the collectivity of a firm's workers. The community's representatives have the right to participate in management decisions, to audit company books and records, and generally to assure that the workers' actual and prospective interests are being protected.

The educational system is being extensively reorganized. Among the reform's features are a stress on preschool and extrascholastic, including adult, education, on common and terminal secondary education with a vocational focus, on bilingual education for Peru's Quechua- and Aymará-speaking indigenous groups, and on the values of nationalism and solidarity. [See "Children of the Andes: Education in Peru," in Section III, below.]

The social security system, built up piece by piece over a fifty-year period, has been reorganized and rationalized. For those already covered, it provides generous retirement, accident, and health benefits more equitably than before, and it extends coverage to a few new groups, including domestic servants and even artists. And labor legislation has been revised to assure increased job security to the employed.

Each of these reforms transfers resources—present and especially future—from more to less privileged Peruvians. All represent considerable advances over the measures previous Peruvian regimes had been willing or able to undertake. Substantial numbers of Peruvians, surely a majority of those groups whose members have voted in Peru's past national elections, are obtaining more, some significantly more, from the national system than they did prior to the military regime.

Viewed from another perspective, however, the current reforms are at least as noteworthy for their limits as for their advance. The military regime's measures are carried out, if somewhat self-consciously, under the banner of Tupac Amaru, the mestizo leader who headed Peru's main Indian uprising against the Spanish conquerors. But the reforms seem unlikely to affect significantly the fundamental distribution of power and rewards in Peruvian society, i.e., between those already participant in Peru's economy and politics and those (the Indians, generally speaking) still largely excluded from the system's benefits. As . . . Peruvian economists . . . have shown, the income distribution resulting from the laws decreed so far—even if fully implemented —will occur almost exclusively within the top quarter of Peru's income recipients; three quarters of Peru's population is unlikely to be much affected. The great majority of Peruvians will not obtain land because there is not enough to go around. They will not become members of industrial communities because they are not among the aristocracy of Peruvian laborers working in industrial firms of the requisite size. They will not get improved social security benefits because they are not among the privileged minority covered by the "national" scheme, nor will they enjoy job security because they have no steady job to begin with. And the benefits their children get from the educational reform will probably be strictly limited, for on the past record their children are likely to be among the majority of school attenders who drop out before the sixth grade.

The coastal sugar estates, the seizure of which provided the most dramatic earnest of the regime's intent in 1969, poignantly illustrate the reforms' limits. Profits which formerly went to the land-owning families . . . are now largely being distributed among the permanent workers at each plantation. These workers were already before 1968 mostly unionized, politicized, and relatively prosperous; now they are even better off. But seasonal workers on the same estates, not made members of the new cooperatives, are about as badly off as they were before. And they, in turn, are better off than the legion of still landless peasants of the highlands who will not be among the beneficiaries of the agrarian reform.

In short, the military regime is distributing resources and rewards in a more equitable way to those Peruvians already able to make their own demands heard and felt—by strikes, land invasions, votes, or other forms of organized expression. In this sense, the military government is carrying on the process of "segmentary incorporation" Peru's elites have managed for generations: to admit claimants with voice and power into the political and economic system, but on terms that will protect its boundaries and prevent the minority within from being overwhelmed by a coalition of the majority without. The identity and relative influence of those on top has changed somewhat, and that is important. But the process of internal domination continues, and those on the bottom are pretty much the same as before.

Moreover, the regime is not doing things which a revolutionary government might be expected to do, or which Castro's, for example, has done. The regime has not undertaken major tax reforms which would significantly increase the burdens on Peru's middle class. (Income tax exemptions in Peru remain among the highest in South America and gasoline taxes the lowest; at last report a gallon of gasoline in Lima cost but twenty cents!) It has not undertaken an "urban reform," restructuring urban real property holdings, and has announced repeatedly it will not. A commercial reform, promised in 1970, has so far been avoided. Foreign interests in Peruvian banks have been strictly limited, but Peru's major private bank, the Banco de Credito, is still flourishing. Although the regime has hampered and intimidated the press, it has not monopolized the media, nor even closed down the major opposition newspapers perceived as reactionary obstacles. In reforming education, the regime has left Lima's elite private schools largely unrestricted.

Evaluating the Reforms

From all these comments, a reasonably clear characterization of the regime might seem to emerge: a government carrying out the kind of limited changes—within established class and sectoral limits—which the previous Belaúnde regime . . . had promised but generally failed to deliver. Such an interpretation would indeed fit the stereotype that many if not most observers of Peru have tended to form from the very first days of the military regime. Despite the regime's declaration of revolutionary intent from the outset, . . . the general rule that a military regime will maintain the status quo dies hard. Skeptical observers have pointed to such indicators as the regime's recurrent efforts to improve its relations with business leaders, and have periodically drawn the conclusion that "the 'revolution' has run its course."

What this interpretation overlooks, however, is the evidence that, despite the limits of what has so far been done, the thrust of the regime's action has been, and continues to be, not to pull back, nor even to consolidate, but to go farther—or at least to leave open the possibility of further advance.

Consider the reforms so far neglected, for instance. While it is true that tax reform measures have so far been limited mostly to rationalizing and improving the enforcement of existing regulations, income tax rates for middle and upper brackets were raised considerably in 1971; moreover, there are indications—the creation and staffing of a special tax research office, for example—that the regime may be working on eventual, more thorough, tax reforms. Although the regime has repeatedly denied it will undertake an urban reform or nationalize private banks, rumors persist that these steps are under consideration, against a background of previous denials that pension plans would be changed, that the fishmeal sector would be nationalized, and so on. A few "reactionary" newspapers have been allowed to persist so far, but others have been taken over. . . .

The reforms already decreed have in several cases been carried further than at first seemed likely. The agrarian reform's scope has been expanded: by eliminating "private reforms," by excusing small farmers from certain payments, and especially by strongly emphasizing collective and cooperative forms of ownership as well as regional planning. Though seasonal workers have so far been denied equal access to the reform's benefits, the regime has served notice that it will also act to improve their lot.

Likewise, the industrial reform of 1970 is now described by the regime as only a partial (some say transitional) measure to transform that part of the economy still to be organized along capitalist lines. The principle of a "compensation fund" to make income distribution somewhat more equitable within each sector has now been extended to the fishing and mining sectors, and is apparently to be pushed still further. The establishment of the "social property" sector reflects the same intent to redistribute property, at least future property, even more widely.

And so it goes all along the line. Initially largely technical and managerial, the educational reform has become more concerned with basic substantive and structural changes. Increasing emphasis is being given to bilingual education, which, if seriously implemented over a sustained period, could perhaps do more than any other single step to undermine Peru's class and caste divisions. Significant talk of facilitating mass participation did not begin until 1971, but since then there have been first steps to make it possible. Each move to establish improved rapport with businessmen has given way to a new cycle of hostility, confounding those who perceived or predicted a military-bourgeois alliance. And while observers have been debating the regime's attitude toward foreign investment, the government has expropriated, nationalized, or bought out one foreign interest after another.

In sum, the measures adopted within this five-year period seem generally to have become more "radical": more statist, somewhat more redistributive, clearly less tied to traditional capitalism, more concerned with participation—at least at the rhetorical level—and seemingly more oriented to a profound restructuring of Peru's social, economic, and political relations. Though current class and sector limits are obvious, there are indications these may be at least partially transcended. Some even contend that the regime has chosen consciously and wisely to wait before curtailing middle-class prerogatives, that the only way to achieve change in Peru was to enlist middle-class support for an attack on oligarchic privilege, and only later to affect the middle class. Such an interpretation is, up to now, still compatible with the regime's conduct. . . .

Unresolved Issues

Notwithstanding its tendency toward more radical measures, the military regime in Peru has, as noted earlier, left a number of central issues unresolved in its first five years. The extent and form of popular participation, the eventual role of the private economy and of foreign investment, whether and how to extend the benefits of reform substantially beyond Peru's modern and advantaged quarter, and above all what, if anything, will be done to institutionalize the "revolution"—all these remain largely open. They raise a final set of questions: Will the regime continue to radicalize? What problems may it encounter, and how will these affect the course of the "revolution"?

Prediction is hazardous, but a few variables should be examined. A presidential succession occurring soon, for instance, would not only eliminate President Velasco's own influence but would probably weaken the impact of . . . the military group most disposed to further and more fundamental reforms. A succession occurring in 1977 or later, however, would probably find precisely these officers fully in charge of the Peruvian army, with all the leverage that hierarchical superiority would afford.

Continuing relative success in economic management would presumably reinforce the self-confidence of both civilian *técnicos* and their military peers. On the other hand, a strong economic downturn, perhaps as a consequence of international events beyond Peru's control, might bring the regime's current policies into question. Again, timing is crucial. If the Peruvian government can weather the storms immediately ahead, until the expected major expansion of copper and, if all goes well, petroleum exports scheduled for 1976 and ensuing years, its course may well proceed unchallenged. But weathering the storms means, among other things, controlling strong inflationary pressures and restraining labor's demands, not easy tasks. . . .

One major problem arises precisely from the trend this essay underlines. The faster the regime's policies advance toward a more fundamental realignment of Peruvian society, the more likely they are to provoke tensions between the military's political and institutional roles and responsibilities. Signs of distress within the officer corps are already evident on issues like the role of SINAMOS and the campaign against [the newspaper] *El Comercio,* and there are indications that officers' opinions may well have constrained the educational reform. It will require extraordinary political skill by Peru's military rulers to maintain the unity of the armed forces as policies continue to evolve.

A second, related problem concerns the viability of an economy based more every month on the public sector. Satisfactory growth has been achieved since 1970 by constantly increasing the scope and intensity of the state's economic activities. The private sector's earlier dynamism has never recovered and shows few signs of doing so. Whether public enterprises are capable of efficiently developing Peru's resources is by no means certain, however. Tell-tale signs that Peru's bureaucracies are already overloaded have begun to accumulate. The Peruvian regime's legislative feats, however impressive, are largely accomplished; the current and future period of implementation will call upon talents and energies not yet fully tested.

Probably the toughest challenge the Peruvian regime faces is the issue of popular participation. If the great majority of Peruvians continue to feel left out of the "revolution," the regime's capacity to deal with opposition without harsh repression may end, and the vicious circle of violence so far mostly avoided may begin. Expanded participation would also have its costs. Precisely those Peruvians who are most mobilized and best able to participate are those who have pushed the regime hardest, seeking additional gains for themselves. Those who stand to benefit from the government's program, apart from the military-bureaucratic elites which obviously gain the most, are either out to secure an even greater share or, up to now, have been glad to receive what is offered. But they have felt few ties to a government which concedes them benefits but grants them little or no say in deciding how these benefits will be achieved or distributed. The advantages of organizing a political apparatus are obvious to many of the regime's civilian and military strategists, but so are the dangers of strengthening organizations which may acquire interests, aims, and power of their own.

An important experiment is underway in Peru. It tests whether soldiers as rulers can use their power to implement major structural changes sufficient to open the way to equitable and integrated national development, without turning to repression, closing off participation, or merely replacing a civilian "oligarchy" with one in uniform—and without undermining the military institution itself. How this experiment fares may influence not only the immediate future of Peru, but the tendency of politics in much of South America, and perhaps elsewhere in the Third World.

URUGUAY'S LOST PARADISE [5]

In 1950, when the Korean war was about to give a
sharp upward boost to agricultural commodity prices, Uruguay was completing more than four decades of political
stability, enjoying satisfactory economic development and
one of the most advanced welfare systems in the world. The
nation's two and a quarter million people enjoyed the third
highest standard of living in Latin America, higher than
that of several European countries, and almost on a level
with Japan. Montevideo's meat packing plants processed
a record 342,000 metric tons of beef that year, leaving
enough, after a staggering home consumption of 176
pounds per capita, for a record 63,000 metric tons of exports.

Exiles from war and dictatorship elsewhere in South
America and Europe found a haven in Uruguay, attracted
by the country's prosperous economy (with a hard-cur-
rency peso pegged at two to the dollar), political stability
and an atmosphere of freedom and content. In a long list
of statistics—a life expectancy of over sixty-five years, newspaper circulation, percent enrolled in higher education,
maternal and infant health—Uruguay was first or second
in Latin America. Foreigners wrote books entitled *Utopia
in Uruguay* and spoke of "The Switzerland of South
America"; *Uruguayos* themselves proudly quoted the national slogan, *"Como Uruguay, no hay"* (There's no country like ours).

. . . [However], after two decades of economic and political misfortune and mismanagement, only a few fragments
of that glowing heritage remain. True to her democratic
traditions, Uruguay carried out a peaceful, open, and hon-
est presidential and congressional election in November
1971. Despite some restrictions on civil liberties (several
newspapers were closed; a few hundred political prisoners

    [5] From article by Samuel Shapiro, writer on Latin American affairs. *Current
History.* 62:98-103. F. '72. Reprinted by permission.

were held without trial), the nation remains vastly freer than Brazil and Argentina, the immensely larger military dictatorships that border her on the north and west. The gross national product of nearly $2 billion, though stable or declining in recent years, is still one of the highest per capita in Latin America; and it is much more equitably distributed than it is anywhere else in the hemisphere. But every measurable statistic and every informal attempt to describe Uruguay's national mood indicate a downward spiral into underdevelopment, distrust and despair. In 1969, Uruguayan government officials themselves had to ask shamefacedly that the Latin American Free Trade Association (LAFTA) classify them as "underdeveloped," along with such economic laggards as Peru, Ecuador and Bolivia.

Uruguay's domestic tranquillity, once so attractive to tourists, exiles and refugees, has been disrupted by an unceasing wave of strikes, demonstrations, riots, guerrilla raids, prison breaks and political kidnappings and murders. The peso, once a desirable hard currency, has been repeatedly and disastrously devalued, from two to the dollar in 1950 to 11 to 1 in 1962, 65 to 1 in 1965, 100 to 1 in 1967, and 250 to 1 in April, 1968; between 1955 and 1970 Uruguay endured an inflation of *9,000* percent. Because of sharp declines in volume and prices for her exports of beef, wool and wheat, Uruguay's gross national product fell 15 percent between 1956 and 1968, and the once proud little republic thus had the worst inflation and the lowest rate of economic growth in the hemisphere.

The 1964 census (the first since 1908, in itself a sign of governmental incompetence) destroyed some illusions. Uruguayans thought they had 3.2 million people, 90 percent literate; they discovered that there were only 2.5 million, of whom 289,000 had never been to school, with another 1 million who had not progressed beyond the sixth grade. Immigration, which had produced a society 90 percent European and 8 percent mestizo (mixed European and Indian) had ceased, and people were leaving the country in increasing numbers. . . . And it was the youngest, best educated and economically most valuable people who were leaving, fleeing the stagnant, depressing bleakness of an economy that could offer them no jobs.

With an estimated 150,000 abortions a year, Uruguay had the lowest birthrate (21 per 1000), the lowest rate of population growth (1.2 percent), and the oldest population in the hemisphere; there are more Uruguayans over fifty years of age than under. The causes of the rise and subsequent decline of the welfare state on the eastern shore of the Uruguay are interesting and important beyond the diminutive republic's borders.

The Batlle Regime

Modern Uruguay was created by the remarkable politician and social reformer José Batlle y Ordóñez (president 1903-1907, 1911-1915). When Batlle arrived on the scene, Uruguay was no different from the other Latin nations, economically backward and divided, heavily in debt, a prey to political upheavals and civil war. In the seventy-three years between 1830 and 1903, there were twenty-five governments, most of them illegitimate. Nine were brought down by violence, two by assassination, one by a bullet wound; ten of the remaining thirteen had to fight off major armed revolts.

Batlle, a political genius who dominated his Colorado party and the nation until his death in 1929, ended all that. He crushed the last . . . revolt during his first presidency; there have been none since. With astonishing foresight, Batlle established one of the world's first welfare states before the outbreak of World War I: by the time of his death, Uruguay had free medical care, accident and unemployment insurance, a system of state pensions, the eight-hour day and the forty-four-hour week, and government operated public utilities, radio stations, a fishing fleet, insurance companies, chemical plants, an airline, distilleries, theatres, casinos and hotels. Batlle's innovations were so

successful and his influence was so compelling that long
after his death Uruguay experimented, unsuccessfully, with
one of his pet ideas, a plural executive, with members
serving as president for one year each.

For all his reforming zeal, however, Batlle did not
touch the basis of Uruguay's economic life, the land. He
was a man of Montevideo, the giant city where nearly half
of Uruguay's citizens live, and most of his actions were
taken for the benefit of the urban worker and the middle
class; he thought the problem of agricultural inefficiency
and rural poverty could be left to take care of itself. Since
neither the Colorados nor the landowner-dominated opposition party Blancos have ever pressed for agrarian reform, five hundred families currently own or operate 8.2
million hectares, half the farmland in the country, and control 70 percent of the wool clip.

The great haciendas, though they have some of the
finest land in the continent, are very badly run, with a
minimum investment in machinery, fertilizer and modern
methods of management. Uruguayan sheep, for example,
produce only 2.9 kilos of wool apiece, as against 3.9 kilos
in Australia and 4.5 in New Zealand. Similarly, it takes 27
Uruguayan cattle to produce a ton of beef; better breeds
and better feeds yield a ton of beef for every 17 cattle in
Argentina, 15 in the US, 13 in Holland. Falling prices and
stagnant agricultural output (beef production reached its
peak in 1950, and wool output in 1954) have undermined
the basic export economy which paid for Uruguay's imports and the urban welfare state. . . .

Economic Crisis

Between the outbreak of World War II in 1939 and
the end of the Korean war in 1953, the basic weaknesses of
the Uruguayan economy were concealed by high export
prices and the growth of a home industry shielded from
foreign competition by wartime conditions and high tariffs.
But although the number of factories in Uruguay increased

from 15,000 in 1938 to 30,000 in 1961, and one fifth of the labor force is in manufacturing and construction, Uruguayan products like textiles, chemicals and pharmaceuticals are high-cost, uncompetitive items that cannot be exported even to neighboring Brazil and Argentina. A small plastics industry survives, for example, only because there is a 225 percent tariff on imported plastic containers, plus an import deposit of 200 percent more, in addition to irregular but frequent foreign exchange control regulations and import bans that shut off competition.

With a home market of less than 3 million people, an enfeebled agricultural sector that buys little machinery, fertilizer or consumer goods, and few native raw materials (Uruguay has no coal, oil, iron or aluminum), Uruguayan industrialists run inefficient, low-productivity plants and depend on government favors for their continued existence. Concentration of power is as great (or greater) in industry as it is in agriculture: 3.6 percent of the industrialists control 74 percent of industrial output. Like the great landowners with whom they are allied in marriage and in politics, Uruguay's businessmen are too often incompetents who want the financial rewards of entrepreneurship without the hard and intelligent risk taking that ought to earn them.

The long-term economic crisis called for considerable belt tightening, agrarian reform, and a cutback in Uruguay's remarkably generous pension laws. Succeeding generations of politicians have reduced the retirement age to 55 or 50; members of the armed forces may retire as early as 32 if they have put in 15 years of service, and women with children can retire on a reduced pension after only 10 years. At age 55, 1 in 3 Uruguayan workers is retired, and there are presently 350,000 pensioners to be supported by an active population of less than 1 million. . . . Another 230,000 government employees, many of them severely underemployed, take 75 percent of the government budget; 19 of the 22 government corporations currently lose money. PLUNA, the government airline, is a good example of bureaucratic waste and inefficiency. Between 1958 and 1966, as the number of operational airplanes fell from 9 to 6, the payroll rose from 700 to 1,000; PLUNA has more employees per plane than any other airline in the world.

Some of the remedies for these problems are obvious, and have been patiently pointed out by foreign and native economists for decades. But in a democracy not faced by foreign war or another obvious crisis situation it is very difficult to take away benefits people have grown to expect, and to which they feel entitled. Blancos and Colorados alike have felt it psychologically unpalatable and politically impossible to tell their countrymen the truth: that they are living beyond their means, not working hard enough, retiring too early, and aspiring to consume without producing. They have resorted instead to demagogy, promises, borrowing abroad . . . and inflation.

In the wake of the continuing economic crisis the party system deteriorated, and the once fairly clear ideological differences between the Colorados (Batlle's party of the urban workers and the middle class) and the Blancos (the rural *hacendados*) melted away. In 1958, and again in 1962, the Blancos won, after ninety-three years in opposition, but proved incapable of effective government under the multiple executive system then in effect. In 1966, a new constitution restored the presidential system, and a Colorado president, retired General Oscar Gestido, returned his party to power.

Political Difficulties

Gestido, who had begun reform as administrator of PLUNA and of the nation's railroads, told his countrymen the truth: "Uruguay is in a mess. But with common sense we can straighten it out." He made a promising beginning, with crackdowns on speculators, a tough approach to strikers, and a war against smuggling (it is estimated that more than one third of Uruguay's imports enter the country illegally, across the river from Argentina or over the accessible border with Brazil). But after only nine months in office Gestido died of a heart attack, mourned even by his political enemies as a nearly indispensable man. He was replaced by Vice President Jorge Pacheco Areco, a little-known editor and career politician who had been nominated—as US Vice Presidents often are—in an obscure political deal.

Pacheco seized the reins of office with more vigor than skill. Within weeks he closed *Epoca* and *El Sol,* two leftist opposition newspapers, and outlawed the Socialists and three other minor parties. In lieu of a structural reform of the economy, he resorted to wage freezes and repeated devaluations, meeting labor protest by drafting strikers (there were seven hundred strikes during his first year in office) and imposing a state of emergency that allowed him to censor and close newspapers and imprison hundreds of leftists without trial. The four years and three months of his term . . . have seen an intensification of the national crisis: skyrocketing prices, long lines for meat and milk, soaring rents that the middle class cannot afford, factory closings, and unemployment of over 15 percent. As one despairing businessman put it: "This country is not to be taken seriously. We have no way out, we have no future. We may just as well consume everything we have, and then wait for the Americans to come and help us out."

The most ominous result of this mood of helplessness and distrust has been the rise of the Tupamaros, an urban guerrilla force of some one thousand to two thousand middle-class students, professionals and disgruntled bureaucrats that has succeeded in making the government look contemptible and ridiculous. Beginning as a sugar cane cutters' union organized in 1960 by Raul Sendic, a former law student, the Tupamaros moved to Montevideo late in 1963. Some of their early tactics were an annual "Poor People's March" on the capital, a raid on a Swiss rifle club in July 1963, and the hijacking of a delivery van and turning its contents over to the slum dwellers of the Aparicio Saravia district on Christmas Eve, 1963.

Under Pacheco, the Tupamaros turned to more violent measures: bank robberies, destruction of business property (especially foreign-owned), seizures of radio stations, canteens, markets, movie theatres and army barracks for brief harangues against the regime, and the seizure of business records from offices and private homes with subsequent publication to expose fraud, tax evasion, and the dishonesty of public officials. . . .

One of the Tupamaros' most effective tactics has been political kidnapping, to raise funds through ransom and to demonstrate the government's inability to protect its own officials. . . . Tupamaro activity has damaged an already feeble economy by frightening off potential investors and ruining the important tourist business on Uruguay's lovely beaches; in 1971, the number of foreign visitors dropped from 300,000 to 200,000, and foreign-exchange revenue from tourism fell over 30 percent. Chaos and confusion are welcomed and promoted by the Tupamaros, who argue that everything must get worse until the Uruguayan people see the necessity and the inevitability of an armed revolution.

A New Coalition

A more sensible, political response to Blanco-Colorado collusion and incompetence has been the formation of a new coalition to challenge the old parties. The Christian Democrats, never as important in two-party Uruguay as they are in some other Latin nations, joined with the Socialists, Communists, and dissident Blancos and Colorados in the Frente Amplio (Broad Front) to contest the 1971 presidential, congressional, and provincial elections. . . .

In the elections . . . the traditional Uruguayan politics of no consecutive reelection for presidents and Colorado-Blanco domination held good. . . . The Broad Front ran far behind, but made an impressive showing in view of the fact that it was organized less than a year before and had to combat political habits and loyalties that are more than a century old. . . .

[Juan M.] Bordaberry [who was elected president] was a member of the outgoing administration which had been unable to find solutions for Uruguay's grave social and economic problems. His campaign was largely a negative one, asking his countrymen to vote against communism rather than for any program of reform and change. . . .

Uruguay's future . . . remains as uncertain as ever. Despite the crumbling of public confidence in recent years, the nation still has the advantages it began with: democratic traditions, a homogeneous, intelligent population, good soils and a temperate climate. If the *Uruguayos* and their leaders can find the inspiration for Batlle-like reforms and the courage to carry them out, the little republic may well recover the ease and well-being of former days. If not, either the Frente Amplio (as in Chile), or the Tupamaros (as in Cuba) may inaugurate a still more radical-revolutionary break with the existing system. And in view of the Tupamaros' known connections with similar groups in Argentina and Brazil, any success they may have in establishing some form of dual government could have grave consequences for the rest of the southern continent and for the US.

PEACE AT A PRICE IN PARAGUAY [6]

Latin America's most durable dictatorship has lasted so long that most Paraguayans were not even born when General Alfredo Stroessner took power.

"We have governed under a reign of peace in a world around us that is shaken by violence," President Stroessner has often reminded his people.

[6] From "Stroessner Gives 'Peace' to Paraguay, but at a Price," article by Jonathan Kandell, correspondent. New York *Times.* p. 2. Ja. 21, '75. © 1975 by The New York Times Company. Reprinted by permission.

Paraguay has escaped the turmoil of political instability, military coups and guerrilla movements that has affected all her neighbors over the last decade. But since taking power in 1954, General Stroessner has continually repressed even moderate voices of dissent and presided over an exodus of almost a million poverty-stricken Paraguayans.

Today, this landlocked, California-sized nation stands on the threshold of an economic windfall, thanks to the construction of a multibillion-dollar hydroelectric project on the Brazilian border that will be five times the size of Egypt's Aswan Dam.

Corruption Is Pervasive

But because of a vast web of corruption that has enveloped the armed forces, politicians and businessmen during the last generation, there are widespread fears that even an infusion of this scope will not be able to set the country on a road of stable, evenly distributed economic growth.

Although military governments are now the rule throughout the hemisphere, the Stroessner regime resembles more closely the personalized, feudalistic dictatorships of a bygone era.

Roads, plazas, schools, an airport and a city are named after him. His portrait, showing him with a trace of a smile and wearing a conservative business suit, hangs in every government office, most stores and even in the living rooms of political opponents.

The Colorado party he heads is a fraternity that draws university students into the bureaucracy and steers businessmen to the "right" political contacts. The army—which was his road to power—is the other pillar of his regime.

Though he has made himself into a monument, General Stroessner at sixty-two maintains a stiff, Teutonic appearance and a hard-driving schedule that exhausts even his younger aides.

A Long Working Day

When he is in the tree-shaded, subtropical capital, the president arrives at his offices at 6 A.M. and often stays late into the night. Every Tuesday, he holds court to a legion of citizens bringing him their grievances, large and small.

But General Stroessner is a man of the provinces, born in the small town of Encarnación, on the Argentine border southeast of Asunción. He spends a good deal of his time in the countryside to be on hand for the opening of a small school, a new bridge, a government office or just to hand out high-school diplomas.

"We are legitimately proud to have cemented the foundations of our democracy, in order to guarantee individual and collective rights," said the president . . . [in one of his speeches].

The country does have a constitution that spells out democratic guarantees. The press occasionally publishes articles critical of the regime's conduct. Opposition slates appear in elections even if they are won by General Stroessner and his Colorados by suspiciously lopsided 80 percent majorities that always spark charges of fraud. A legislature meets and minority congressmen often heatedly denounce government actions.

But there is a catch. Ever since General Stroessner took power, the country has been in a constant state of siege, under which all constitutional guarantees are suspended. Even though the president controls the court system after a generation of patronage, justice is often meted out by the ubiquitous secret police—known as *"pyragues,"* meaning "people with hairy feet."

Detained One Hundred Times

In his office overlooking the purple-blossomed jacaranda trees of a lower-middle-class neighborhood, the president of the small, moderate Christian Democratic party recently celebrated his realease after his one-hundredth detention.

"Most of the times, they held me only a few hours," said Luis Alfonso Resck, a small, wiry former university professor. "Sometimes it lasted a few months. Once they kept me in a village so isolated that during the rainy season there was no way to get there." . . .

Imprisonment and torture seem to be the credentials of most opposition party leaders.

Carmen Lara Castro, a congresswoman and president of the Human Rights Commission, has been imprisoned, and her husband as well. Their son was tortured.

"I was a prisoner nineteen times and I was tortured six times," said Senator Carlos Levi Rufinelli, a leader of the Liberal party, a conservative group. "Most of the time, I did not know what they wanted. . . .

Plot Is Charged

Repression in Paraguay comes in waves, sometimes reaching high tide, sometimes receding. . . . [Early in 1975] —ever since the government claimed to have discovered a student-led plot against General Stroessner and other ranking officials—detentions have been numerous and charges of brutality widespread.

According to Mrs. Lara Castro, about two hundred people are under detention for political reasons, and several hundred more were jailed briefly.

"People are used to hardship and brutality," she said. "Abroad, why should people care with much of the same happening in Chile and Uruguay and Brazil? Here, there are people who walk ten miles and say it's not far. I know a person who was tortured and said the man who picked him up wasn't a bad fellow because he gave him advice on how to hold up."

Her husband paced the hallway and the living room, while her son occasionally peered nervously from the inner patio, but Mrs. Lara Castro, a pleasant middle-aged woman, seemed at ease.

"I keep fighting because it would be treason to stop after all that has happened," she said. "Then also, I have been doing this sort of work most of my life. I used to take the kids when I visited friends and political prisoners in jail. They would study their school lessons in the car while I went inside."

In his last Christmas message, the archbishop of Asunción, the Most Rev. Ismael Rolón, denounced "the use of torture as the normal method of extracting confessions."

Officials Excommunicated

The archbishop's charges may have marked the beginning of another period of strained relations between the church and the government. In the late sixties, Roman Catholic bishops and priests called for a restoration of civil liberties, agrarian reform and an end to corruption.

A few priests were jailed and allegedly tortured. The beating of a visiting Uruguayan bishop in 1971 by government-led demonstrators led to the excommunication of several public officials, including the minister of interior and the chief of police.

After a visit to the Vatican by President Stroessner two years ago, relations between the clergy and the government seem to improve. Archbishop Rolón lifted the excommunications in September [1974].

But in his last public message, the archbishop denounced "the spectacle of a privileged few who accumulate ostentatious riches by any means while the majority, in the cities and especially in the countryside, are engaged in a daily struggle for survival."

War-Decimated Population

With a long history of violence and plunder, Paraguay remains one of the most backward nations in Latin America. A disastrous war against Argentina, Uruguay and Brazil from 1865 to 1870 reduced the country's population from 525,000 to 221,000—with only about 28,000 men among the survivors.

The Chaco War against Bolivia in the 1930s left 100,000 Paraguayans dead, and a civil war in 1947 claimed a few thousand more lives.

Today, the per capita income is about $300 a year, but even this low figure does not take into account the unequal distribution of the meager wealth.

The two universities have only about 10,000 students between them. Illiteracy is estimated to be around 50 percent, with a third of the population speaking only the Guaraní Indian language.

With only about 1,100 doctors for a population of about 2.5 million, Paraguay has an infant-mortality rate that is among the highest in the hemisphere, and the vast majority of Paraguayans suffer from intestinal viruses, according to the government's secretariat of national planning.

The broad, meandering Paraguay River, the lush vegetation in the streets and brick-tile colonial houses give Asunción a timeless tranquillity unlike any other Latin American capital.

Asunción is largely devoid of the slums that ring almost every other city on the continent, because with few urban jobs available, the country has escaped the postwar rural migration that has affected the rest of Latin America, but Argentina has drawn almost a million impoverished Paraguayans to her urban shantytowns.

More than 60 percent of Paraguayans still live in the rural interior, often in villages devoid of machines where the only sounds are the creaking of oxcarts and the dull thud of machetes clearing crops and underbrush.

Tribes Losing Battle

To the north and west of her capital, in the Chaco, a shrub-covered wilderness where summer temperatures reach over 100 degrees, a few thousand Mennonite farmers have maintained a nineteenth century way of life. Close to the more fertile plains of the Paraguay River, an Argentine family has carved out a rural empire extending over seven million acres.

In the jungles east of Asunción close to the Brazilian border, stone-age hunting tribes are fighting a losing battle against the onslaughts of land-hungry white settlers and assimilated Indians.

The economic hope of the country lies in the construction of a $3 billion hydroelectric project along the Paraná River on the Brazilian border. The Itaipu complex will be the largest dam in the world.

When completed in the 1980s—largely through Brazilian capital and technical know-how—it will meet Paraguay's electricity needs and earn the country an estimated $130 million yearly through sales of electric power to Brazil.

The prospect of heavy investment has already created a lawless, gold-rush atmosphere along the border. The rich red earth near the Paraná River has attracted 50,000 Brazilian colonists. Their wooden shacks and tin-roofed houses dot the countryside and muddy roads where jungle brush has only recently been cleared.

About 500 Paraguayan farmers, squatters who lived for years without land titles, have been displaced by Paraguayan Army officers who were deeded properties near the Itaipu site supposedly for "reasons of national security."

The Land is Resold

"After a while," explained a displaced squatter, Favio Ramirez, "we found out that the officers bought the lands for 1,000 guaranis a hectare with ten years to pay. Then they turned around and sold it to the Brazilian colonizing companies for 15,000 guaranis a hectare." A hectare is about 2.5 acres and 1,000 guaranis represent about $8.

The armed forces and police have repeatedly been accused of tolerating and participating in the widespread

smuggling that has stunted the growth of Paraguay's industry and commerce.

Last year, during a promised crackdown on contraband,
police stopped a caravan bringing $260,000 worth of
smuggled consumer goods from Brazil. Opposition legisla-
tors denounced the smuggler as a chaplain in the armed
forces.

Entire blocks of stores in Asunción are stocked with
smuggled goods. Street markets . . . subsist on the contraband trade.

III. DEVELOPMENT IN PERSPECTIVE

EDITOR'S INTRODUCTION

South America, though relatively much better off economically than Africa or Asia, still faces many grave development problems. Millions of people in South America are living at a subsistence level in appalling slums with few sanitary facilities. Housing is grossly substandard, often consisting of homemade structures built of scraps. As a result of malnutrition and poor medical facilities, there is an extremely high rate of mortality among the children of the poor.

At the same time, there are important positive factors to brighten the picture. Some countries, such as Brazil and Venezuela, are industrializing rapidly, thus creating jobs. Several countries have initiated substantial social welfare programs. The United Nations, the World Bank, and other groups, as well as individual governments, have been quietly working with the South American countries in a joint effort to solve the region's pressing development problems.

This section considers the issues of development by recounting what several assistance groups are doing in various countries. The first three selections review the efforts of the United Nations Children's Fund (UNICEF) in Peru, Colombia, and Paraguay. They vividly show how much there is to be done, how difficult and slow the work is, and how the local authorities are taking an active part in cooperation with international efforts.

A major obstacle to orderly economic growth is the region's staggering and chronic inflation. How South Americans have tried to cope with ever mounting prices is the subject of the next report.

The following selection analyzes the special position of Brazil, the "colossus of the south," feared by some as a potential imperialist power with the entire continent as its sphere of influence.

The final article covers some of the activities of the World Bank Group in Argentina, Bolivia, Brazil, and Colombia. Many World Bank loans are given at a low interest rate ($\frac{3}{4}$ of 1 percent); others are given at commercial terms because they are expected to generate enough revenue so that repayment with interest can begin at an early date. Some loans are for infrastructure—such as improving transportation networks or expanding electric power capacity. Other loans are for improving, diversifying, or expanding agriculture or for improvements in such fields as industry and education. As can be seen from this excerpt, hundreds of millions of development dollars have been poured into the South American countries. Some of the loans have already begun to bring dividends to the recipients. But so vast are the development problems that huge additional sums are necessary.

CHILDREN OF THE ANDES: EDUCATION IN PERU[1]

An idea far more revolutionary than the drastic land-reform decrees introduced in Peru by the military government after the 1968 coup d'état was one concerning children—that education should start in the cradle and not in the classroom.

So determined was the revolutionary government to introduce drastic educational reforms to parallel the sweeping agrarian reforms that it gave the measure equally high priority, despite the misgivings of some critics. In fact, the special Commission for Educational Reform, which began work shortly after the new regime was installed, had to endure many jokes at its own expense. Some teachers asked if they would have classes of newborn babies, others if they

[1] From "Children of the Andes," article by Alastair Matheson, deputy director of information, United Nations Children's Fund. *UNICEF News.* Issue 80 (1974/2):4-10. '74.

were expected to be nurses instead of educators. A few even mockingly inquired if they were expected to give toilet training in the new curriculum.

The Peruvian government soon showed it was no joke, but a policy to be applied in deadly earnest, as part of a deliberate strategy to wrest power from the landed oligarchy of that time and place it in the hands of the people, creating a more egalitarian society. The measures were aimed especially at bringing the Indian population of Peru more into the mainstream of public life and to ensure that they were no longer an underprivileged group, as had been the case ever since Pizarro and the conquistadors crushed the Incas' power early in the sixteenth century. (Indians today constitute one half of Peru's 12 million population.)

As the very first rung in the ladder of the new educational system devised after careful study, the reform commission recommended that the process of "initial education" should begin, if not actually at birth, at least within one year of the child's life. The intention is that this will shape the formative mind so that by the time formal schooling begins at six years of age, the child will be able to take the maximum advantage of it.

"A Waiting Period"

To understand the hoped-for far-reaching consequences of the new policy in Peru, it is important to realize that throughout the days of Spanish colonial rule, and ever since, Peruvians have tended to look upon childhood as a "waiting period," when the child is more or less left alone, with little effort made by the parents at preparation for the life ahead. Only once the age of six has been reached, has it been considered necessary to do anything about developing the young mind.

Members of the military government felt that the traditional system worked unfairly to the advantage of the children of the privileged few, by the mere fact that the surroundings of a rich home and family are more conducive

to learning and mental stimulation, while the peasants—
mainly the Indians—suffered from the delay in learning.

Some sociologists have described the Indians' present
aloofness, apathy, and reluctance to take part in the life
and development of Peru as deriving, in part, from delayed
education—coupled with a system which instilled into the
poorer people from a very early age a sense of humility and
subservience, owing to undue emphasis upon such words
as "respect," "order" and "discipline."

"In the former Peruvian society, childhood meant something like an incomplete human form, a young person in
an immature condition." These are the words of . . . one
of the most outspoken critics of the old system, a former
civil servant who is now highly regarded as a leading educator. . . . As a strong advocate of the new educational
policy, he defends it this way:

> Until poverty can be eradicated in Peru, the poor children
> which are now in the majority, must be helped through a multi-
> sectoral educational program of initial education. Any educational
> effort which does not include the child between birth and five
> years of age will be fruitless, for attention provided after this
> period is too late.
> The basic elements which the young child must have are
> adequate nutrition, family love, understanding and security, the
> happenings and experiences which produce early stimulation,
> plus preventive care. Those components already exist in most
> privileged Peruvian homes where the availability of proteins,
> vitamins, medical care, educational toys, travel and music, are in
> direct proportion to the income of the family. It is not so in
> the case of the peasant farmer or the factory worker, or even
> worse, of the unemployed. Their small incomes lead them to the
> tragic vicious circle that blocks their children's development.

Keystone of Policy

Although all educators do not accept the concept that
a delayed start in schooling can cause irreparable damage
to a child's mental development, nevertheless the revolutionary government in Peru has accepted it without reser-
vation and it forms the keystone of the nation's "initial

education" policy, which is now the start of the entire educational system—described as "a birth-to-death process."

The new policy has been based on the report of the
Commission for Educational Reform. This maintained that
sociologists, psychologists, and doctors had found that a
child's intelligence in the first six years of life remained at
a low level and even atrophied if it did not have the chance
of sharing varied and enriching social experiences. "As this
possibility is denied to children from diminished socioeconomic groups, those children are precisely the ones
which suffer in their early childhood from psychological
and mental blockage. . . . When school starts, it is frequently too late, as the handicaps already are difficult to
compensate for."

The commission argued that the arduous efforts which
such children made to reach normal levels at school were
often the source of new tensions which eventually led to
some children running away from school. Those who remained at school tended to isolate themselves from others
who had been more fortunate and enjoyed more adequate
experiences in early childhood, bringing with them the
so-called "hidden curriculum" denied to those from the
deprived groups.

Despite the urgent recommendations contained in the
first report of the commission issued in 1969, it was not
until 1972 that the government promulgated its new law
on educational reform, as further research and study had
to be undertaken. The new law introducing the policy of
initial education opened up many exciting prospects for
educators in Peru, third largest country in Latin America.
It also opened the way for special assistance from UNICEF
in support of the new policy.

Pilot Project Among Indians

One early development was the introduction of a pilot
project for initial education among the children of the
Agaruana Indians living along the banks of the Marañón

River after its long plunge down from the Andean snows into the Amazonas Region. In this area of eastern Peru, where one of the largest Indian communities lives, parents are now being actively involved in the early education of their children, and eventually this duty will become the responsibility of the entire community.

In addition to the parents themselves, young couples who have not yet had any children of their own and even students still completing their education are also being involved, so that all can become "multipliers" of the new concept.

So that health and nutritional standards can be improved concurrently with educational standards, "health promoters" and "nutrition promoters" are being trained to go into the countryside to persuade parents to create school gardens and produce more nutritious food. They are also encouraging local carpenters and village craftsmen to make educational toys which will serve as aids to teaching manual skills and manipulative dexterity to young pre-school children.

UNICEF Participation

UNICEF has already delivered equipment for education centers to this remote community which lies on the far side of the Andes from Lima and the coast. Other supplies also sent include workshop tools, garden equipment, and some educational toys to serve as prototypes for local craftsmen to copy for the project, which was scheduled for full operation in April 1974.

I was able to gain a good impression of the concept behind "initial education" on a visit to the Andean town of Huaraz, in the heart of the zone devastated by the earthquake of 1970 and nestling in the shadows of twenty-thousand-foot peaks. As part of UNICEF's contribution to the national reconstruction effort, three "integrated service modules" have been equipped in Huaraz itself, with another in the fishing port of Chimbote. The fourth is in the village of

Chasquitambo, half way up the steep, twisting track which climbs from the coast up to twelve thousand feet and then down to Huaraz. Two more are planned.

These "integrated modules" are the practical application of the initial education concept, and also put into practice the idea of close cooperation between the Ministries of Education and Health for child development. Special funds were provided by UNICEF committees in the USA and Denmark for this project.

On arrival at the Centro del Salud (Health Center) of Huarupampa, a section of Huaraz, I found seventy youngsters ranging in age from six months to six years. In one brightly-decorated room sixteen infants were asleep in their cots, oblivious of the clatter which came from the neighboring room containing two- and three-year-olds seated at tables, busily scribbling away with pencils or daubing paints on paper. A few were engrossed in building blocks and various educational toys.

Outside I could hear the excited shouts of a group of four- and five-year-olds. The boys were deeply involved in a game of soccer which moved swiftly over the ample but far-from-smooth playing field, but the girls ignored the action, as they played with their dolls while the less "conformist" were building something with full-size "bricks" which turned out to be made from cardboard.

Presiding over this varied assortment of children—all bursting with energy despite the thin air of two-miles-high Huaraz—was Carmen Pongo Huaman, a dynamic twenty-five-year-old *educator familiar,* or social worker, in charge of the project.

Incas' Descendants

Switching effortlessly from her native Spanish to fluent English acquired during a recent two-year tour of study at Sacramento, California, Carmen pointed out that there was great competition for places in the center, but that only children needing special care which their parents were unable to provide were given places. Admission was based on family circumstances, needs and physical condition, she emphasized in between snatches of conversation in the local Indian language, Quechua, which is spoken by these young descendants from the Incas, few of whom understand Spanish.

What is unique about Huarupampa and the four other "modules" of the Andean Reconstruction Zone is the fact that the children are under constant medical supervision, not only from a couple of nurses, but also from a full-time doctor and a dentist. Attached to each school is the health center, which has the additional functions of meeting the needs of the people of the neighborhood, and keeping a check on the diet of the children to ensure they get their proper quota of proteins in their school meals.

The children who attend those "integrated services modules" have ample opportunity for mental stimulation as well as for physical recreation in cheerful, airy surroundings, with a staff which takes great care of their well-being. At the same time, the mothers who are released temporarily from responsibility for the children are expected to use the extra time at their disposal to benefit themselves and their families.

What is now happening at Huaraz will soon, if the government's plans are fully implemented, spread throughout Peru. Teachers will be expected to take on the dual job of being promoters as well as educators, with education changing from a highly centralized formal system to a community-controlled *núcleo,* where the teacher is not only an educator of children but becomes a catalytic agent to awaken the abilities of children and also adolescents and adults in stimulating the self-help spirit.

Criticisms Listed

It is an ambitious plan with many problems still unsolved, but the planners hope to see full implementation by 1980. In the meantime, a series of seminars and education workshops which UNICEF has helped to organize have already produced some trenchant criticisms of the slow progress so far achieved. Among the problems spotlighted by the Seminar on Initial Education, held in Lima in September 1973, were the following:

(1) There is still not enough coordination between government ministries and with private organizations concerned with children's development.

(2) Universities have not taken an active enough role and have tended to "remain aloof," not modifying their curricula to allow for training in initial education.

(3) The mass media, which was expected to participate in helping to change parental attitudes and that of the community as a whole towards responsibilities for educating children, has not yet become involved. Commercial television programs in particular are considered lacking in any educational value and are, in fact, an alienating influence, since they do not stimulate creativity in children or guide parents' attention to the basic needs of childhood. The seminar report accused them of "converting the population into passive recipients of foreign ideologies and ways of living which are incompatible with the national reality."

(4) There has been no research about young children, especially into the differences in the various ecological regions of the country. The seminar recommended that studies should be made regarding the types of games which children play, playing preferences of children, the "sociabilization" of children at different levels in Peru, and the whole question of their psychological evolution.

(5) Finally, it was felt that too much stress had been laid on the five-year-olds in kindergartens and not enough on developing day-care centers for younger children.

It is, therefore, evident that in spite of the bold start, much still remains to be done in getting initial education off to a good start in Peru, where education is taking on a new and more scientific approach, less paternalistic than in the past. It is aimed at helping the underprivileged majority of children, linking school education to mother and child care, also with adequate nutrition and the early stimulation of children during their first, formative years of life.

Science Teaching

Meanwhile, at the other end of the educational ladder, considerable progress can be reported as far as the introduction of science teaching and the use of science equipment are concerned. Much of this has been due to the initiative shown by PRONAMEC (a program for the improvement of science teaching) in developing locally designed and locally produced teaching equipment. This has also been made possible with the help of UNICEF and UNESCO through seminars, workshops and the provision of prototype equipment and production material.

In Peru in the past, even science teachers have not had any equipment with which to conduct experiments and most of the learning had to be confined to theory from textbooks. Things are changing now, with a number of ingenious and low-cost items being produced for school use. These include, for example, a simple microscope which costs only eighteen cents to make, a gyroscope made out of a bicycle wheel and even more sophisticated apparatus using microwaves to demonstrate the refraction of light and another to show the effect of waves on the seashore.

At both ends of the educational ladder in Peru, bold and far-sighted initiatives are achieving results and despite the considerable difficulties ahead caused by influences which range from traditional conservatism, ethnic apathy, the heritage of the past and economic pressures, there is a determination that the rising generation will at least enjoy equal opportunity and the past inequalities will be swept away for good.

"CHILDREN FIRST!" IS THE SLOGAN
IN COLOMBIA [2]

At first sight it resembles a shady tree. Closer inspection reveals a pair of green, cupped hands sheltering a family—father, mother and two children. The symbol, familiar all over Colombia, is an apt one for this is just what the Colombian Institute for Family Well-Being (ICBF) is doing—helping to protect families and children, especially the vast numbers of underprivileged.

The institute virtually operates as a "ministry for children" and enjoys full government support as the coordinator of efforts to protect family life in a changing society and works to improve conditions for young people. It leaves scarcely any aspects of child welfare in Colombia uncovered.

In collaboration with 468 other organizations throughout this South American country, the institute works mainly in the densely populated areas but 40 percent of its budget is devoted to the more sparsely populated rural areas and small cities and towns.

The Colombian government has shown intense social consciousness towards the problems of the family and the child. Their efforts over the last five years have been instrumental in producing the institute, which is unique in the region, as it focuses on the family. Its formation a few years ago was linked directly with the conference on family life which UNICEF helped to organize in Colombia in 1970, and it was only natural that the Children's Fund should decide to work through the newly formed institute when it launched its special program of assistance to Colombia under the title of "Selected Services for Children."

Observing some of the ICBF activities in Colombia during a recent visit, I was especially impressed by the motivation and social concern displayed by those Colombians who

[2] From "Children of the Andes," article by Alastair Matheson, deputy director of information, United Nations Children's Fund. *UNICEF News.* Issue 80 (1974/2):10-15. '74.

are trying to come to grips with the numerous social problems. These have arisen mostly as a result of the country's
transition from a mainly agricultural economy to the present
economy which is becoming more and more industrialized.

Two Evils

Two major evils threaten the future of children in
present-day Colombia. One is the tremendous and still growing extent of malnutrition found among the young because
of lack of proteins in the daily diet, coupled with an increasing tendency for nursing mothers to avoid breast feed-
ing. The other evil is gross overcrowding, which is having
the most detrimental effects on family life.

One social worker in a Bogotá slum put it to me suc-
cinctly this way: "The bad diet not only stunts the child's
growth, but can also affect mental development. It is only
too common to find homes where the seeds of social malad-
justment are planted through a combination of malnutrition, loneliness, and parental indifference. . . ."

Drastic Action

Just what is the Institute for Family Well-Being, and
its collaborators all over Colombia, doing about the problem? There are two main programs for helping children, besides a considerable amount of research. One to which the
institute itself gives priority is for social action aimed at preventing any further deterioration of conditions for children.
This is implemented mainly through a chain of children's
community and day-care centers which form the keystone of
the applied nutrition and research operation.

Eventually these will be expanded into "neighborhood
development centers" to become the foci for providing basic
services in health, nutrition, nonformal education and recreation to low-income Colombian families. With considerable help from UNICEF, UNDP (United Nations Development Program) and UNDESA (UN Department of Economic

and Social Affairs), the institute is now actively involved in the detailed planning arrangements.

The aid provided by UNICEF consists of transport training grants for social workers and other personnel, plus equipment. The most recent contribution has been a printing plant which will enable the institute to print a variety of instructional and training manuals at its Bogotá headquarters.

Bogotá Slum

Much work to help children is already in progress in the slums and shantytowns of Colombia's urban areas. Bogotá, the "go ahead" capital of Colombia with its many ancient and modern buildings on the high Andean plateau, also has its share of squalor, misery and neglect—but "conveniently" concentrated in the "poor" southern end. (By coincidence rather than design, this sprawling city which runs from north to south below a mountain ridge, begins in the north with the magnificent residences of rich Bogotans and progresses down the social scale towards the south, terminating in decrepit *barrios* and makeshift shanties which climb up bare hillsides to the city boundary.)

It was to this slum area that I went to see what the institute is doing for the children of poor families congregated there—many of them new arrivals from the countryside still seeking a place and some means of subsistence in their new surroundings. At Tunjuelito I saw something of the institute-backed applied nutrition operation which provides a total of two million children and pregnant women all over Colombia with nourishing food to supplement their ordinary diet. This is one of the health centers which cooperate with the institute in its nutrition research work into the effects of malnutrition in the mental as well as physical development of the young. Its work has attracted worldwide attention and a number of universities are cooperating, including Cornell and Harvard in the US and Giessen in the Federal Republic of Germany.

From the Womb

Research has been going on for four years. At first they measured the growth of children from the age of six months to three years, comparing those who received a dietary supplement with those who did not. Then it was decided that a more accurate comparison could be made if the observations began in the womb itself, and so mothers from the fourth month of pregnancy cooperated by having their food intake carefully checked and then, from the birth of their child, the baby's mental and physical development was recorded up to the age of three years.

The main incentive for the mothers is the free medical attention all receive, but for the purpose of comparison some receive regular dietary supplements for themselves and their children, while others do not. . . .

A Day-Care Center: La Victoria

In another part of the slum-city of southern Bogotá is La Victoria—one of a chain of community/day-care centers which the Institute for Family Well-Being is creating in the capital. The seventy "under-sevens" were enjoying their play period when I visited the center. All are from poor homes where the mother works and they are in need of care.

As in most countries of Latin America today, Colombian experts in child psychology insist that, even if children have to be away from their homes because of property, parental disputes or other causes, every effort should be made to retain family ties. And so, while La Victoria is a busy day-care center in the mornings, in the afternoons and evenings it becomes a community center to which the older brothers and sisters, as well as the fathers and mothers, if they can, are encouraged to attend.

The opportunity is then taken for discussion sessions at which individual family relationships are examined, and instruction given in health, hygiene, nutrition, child care, and family planning to the older members. In cases where a marriage seems on the point of breaking up, counselors try to persuade reconciliation for the sake of the children.

Away from this environment, the institute has a section which devotes its energies to child protection, working closely with a legal department in cases where minors find themselves in courts or committed to reformatories or approved schools. (Social workers in Colombia carefully avoid using the word "delinquents" and the institute refers to them as "exceptional minors.")

Taking the attitude that these offenders (they may be petty thieves, vagrants, pickpockets, members of rowdy teenage gangs or child prostitutes) are not criminals but victims of society and the product of poverty and slum conditions, the social workers try to research the background of each case and recommend one of several options.

Observation Centers

Such children, committed by the courts or referred independently to the care of the institute, are kept at observation centers for a period of diagnosis to check on their social and psychological conditions before recommending action, either through protection or reeducation. This is often done by way of vocational training or similar practical work.

As far as possible, they are provided with medical, psychological and educational care, depending on individual circumstances, and the principal aim being to see that the child is given an opportunity to readjust to a normal and useful life.

The legal department keeps under constant review all legislation affecting children, as well as the large numbers of individual cases where children are involved in legal proceedings, either as minor offenders coming before the courts, or where they are the objects of custodial cases, parenthood or alimony suits. In every instance, the institute tries to seek a solution most beneficial to the children involved, always safeguarding the rights of the child.

Rural areas now unprotected will be the next field of action for the institute through the UNICEF-assisted "Selected Services" program which aims to create better conditions for community development.

Much has been accomplished but a great deal more time will be needed before lasting results can be achieved.

PIONEERING IN PARAGUAY—A NEW PROMISE [3]

Around the Paraguayan frontier town of Choré, little more than a collection of wooden buildings hemmed in by thick subtropical forest less than one hundred miles from the capital city of Asunción, two thousand pioneer families are turning wilderness into productive farmland.

The Choré community is just part of a vast government "colonization" effort—which in the past ten years alone has opened up 10,000 square miles to 400,000 settlers—but it is developing three times faster than other colonies.

Its success has made it a model for a new settlement area to be established around the proposed dam and hydroelectric project on the Alto Paraná River.

Behind Choré's rapid growth is a government experiment to "integrate" rural development—Paraguay's first coordinated attempt to solve the major problems faced by its pioneering program.

To see the real significance of this experiment, it is necessary to understand the reasons behind the Paraguayan colonization program.

Its basic objective is to harness for Paraguay's economic development two of the country's most underutilized assets. The first of these is Paraguay's vast area of unused hinterland; the second, the untapped human resources of the country's *campesino* population—the landless farmers who work small plots of larger estates, crowded into the heavily

[3] From article in *UNICEF News.* Issue 80 (1974/2):29-34. '74. The article is based on a report, edited by Anthony Hewett, of a visit to Choré by photojournalist David Mangurian.

populated central area of the country, lucky to make as much as $100 each a year. Sixty percent of Paraguay's largely rural population lives on only seven percent of its land; and four fifths of the rural population are landless *campesinos*.

Colonization was meant to bring the landless together with the land, winning a double economic advantage.

But pioneering has never been an easy process and Paraguay has proved no exception. With colonization programs completely outpacing the government services needed to get the settlers on their feet, the colonists' unsupported and uncoordinated efforts have taken as much as a decade to reach the hoped-for economic takeoff.

Help from the Outside

It was this situation which in 1971 prompted the National Council of Social Progress, an overall body representing the relevant government ministries and agencies, to launch the experiment, with the help of bilateral and international agencies, including UNICEF, in seven colonies around Choré.

By 1972 a five-year program had begun to provide technical services to the families—a total of 11,000 people—in the area. Within that first year, four agricultural technicians, one agronomist, four auxiliary nurses, a midwife, a sanitation technician, two malaria-control experts, fifteen teachers, two food and nutrition specialists, two coordinators, an agricultural credit supervisor and three Peace Corps volunteers had gone to work there.

Now, the people of the Choré colonies are showing that in two to three years, instead of the usual ten, pioneers can produce and market enough of their crops to ensure not only self-sufficiency, but a contribution to the overall economy of the country.

Turning Jungle Into Farms

In Choré the hardships are at once apparent. The jungle presses in on all sides. It is hot, sometimes 105 degrees, and humid. Mosquitoes are so numerous that, as one settler puts it, it is necessary to eat with one hand and swat with the other.

Settlers are brought in to Choré by government truck and given a fifty-acre plot, which they can buy for $240 over five years. Often the head of the family arrives first, with his brother or eldest son. They live in rooms in Choré until they can build their thatched hut or *pingó,* and clear some of the trees from their plot.

With only a machete or an ax, that's hard work. The trees are hardwoods and it can take several men a month to clear even 2.5 acres.

"One begins to wish," says settler Genaro Sanguina, a slightly-built twenty-year-old, "that the trees will fall down by themselves."

Once an acre is cleared, settlers like Sanguina, with his wife and two-month-old daughter, move into their *pingó,* plant corn, peanuts, beans and mandioca—a starchy root eaten in most of tropical America—and haul their water three quarters of a mile down a muddy road until more land can be cleared and the family put on its feet.

Dealing With the Problems

Before 1972, the only help the settlers got was some sustenance food supply from the World Food Program (WFP) [a United Nations agency which supplies food for development projects]. The government estimated that because of a lack of outside help, the settlers produced only about half their potential output. Family income in the area was averaging only about $400 a year.

One difficulty was lack of the credit needed to buy necessary seeds and tools. Little was available to settlers because the National Development Bank requires a guarantee of land ownership and only a small percentage of colonists had paid off their $240 mortgages.

So another government organization which provides credit to small farmers' associations began operating in the area in mid-1973 with an initial supply of seeds, pesticides and hand tools given by UNICEF. As crops are marketed, and loans repaid, a revolving fund is created to allow credit for more farmers.

By the end of 1973, 312 farmers were members of 14 credit associations. And plans for settlers' cooperatives have followed. There is no government price support for any crop except tobacco so the settlers will have to organize their own strength in fields such as production, consumption, and marketing.

Trucks, Tractors and a Mobile Saw

The necessity for this sort of self-sufficiency has already been demonstrated by the settlers' experience in marketing. Without transport of their own to the outside world, they found themselves at the mercy of truckers who could buy up their crops for low prices. Also, heavy rains close the main road . . . for four months a year with feeder roads impassable even more often. UNICEF estimated 20 to 30 percent of farmers' crops were wasted because they couldn't be marketed. Now the Rural Welfare Institute has bought three trucks to take in the WFP food and bring out crops on the return trip, particularly tobacco, charcoal and an essence of sour orange used in perfume making.

There is still no public transport in the area and hours are wasted walking to stores for day-to-day necessities.

Most farming is done with only hand tools using little pesticide or fertilizer; there are no silos for grain storage and only a few poor tobacco sheds.

UNICEF is providing a tractor to help train young farmers in modern techniques and a mobile saw to help settlers clear their land more efficiently, at the same time making better use of their cut timber. Colonists donate half the lumber for community health and vocational training centers and schools. Local housing is expected to improve, too.

Building Schools and Digging Wells

Meanwhile, health and education are getting attention in the area for the first time. Education faces a hard struggle —30 percent of the area's children don't attend school and most of those who do never get past the third grade. Only 4 percent get to the sixth grade. Barely half the teachers are fully trained.

Now more fully trained teachers are being recruited, and with the help of the US Agency for International Development, more classrooms will be built. UNICEF has equipped school workshops with tools which can also be used by the community and the International Labor Organization has helped to build six community workshops.

Water is a major problem and health hazard. Some colonists have to walk a mile to fetch it. But the sanitation technician has been supervising well digging—done by hand to a minimum depth of 150 feet and sometimes to as much as 200 feet. In 1972, from sixty-three attempts, thirty-seven of these wells proved successful. Now pumps provided by UNICEF will make it easier to bring water up from these wells.

The sanitation engineer is also encouraging latrine-building, boosting the number built from fifty in 1971 to six hundred in 1972.

Improving Cooking, Increasing Protein

A major contribution to improving health in the area has been the Government Food and Nutrition Program (PAEN). Two of its staff have visited settlers' homes, distributing seeds, seedling pines and citrus trees; they have also encouraged the raising of chickens and rabbits and the growing of high-protein soybeans.

This is the heart of the problem, for protein is difficult to obtain . . . ; there is neither meat nor refrigerators to store it. Nor cows to provide milk.

As a result, 10 percent of the settlers are malnourished

and 70 percent are further weakened by intestinal parasites. . . .

With seeds from PAEN, the farmers, many of whom had never eaten vegetables, are now growing beans, tomatoes, corn, peanuts as well as fruits like pineapple, watermelon, strawberries and grapefruits.

Most important of all for the future of the Choré project is the building of community spirit. PAEN is part of this, too, through its fifteen-day courses to help the settlers develop their own leaders. The people have already formed their own committees for such tasks as distributing the supplies provided by the World Food Program. Mothers' clubs are teaching better nutrition and child-feeding practices. The government is beginning to make Choré more of a town.

In just two years, the people of the Choré project—with a little help from their friends—have given pioneering in Paraguay a new level of promise.

CHRONIC INFLATION [4]

Reprinted from *U.S. News & World Report*

Latin Americans have known for more than a century what people in the US are just learning: Once it starts running away, inflation is almost impossible to stop.

And in Latin America, chronic inflation has led to some bewildering results:

☐ Bread in Uruguay now has a strange taste. By law, 10 percent of the flour must be milled from grain sorghums, which are cheaper than wheat. Housewives expected this would keep bread relatively inexpensive. But the price went up another 20 percent in June [1974].

☐ Banks in Argentina are open only between noon and 4 p.m. This allows bank employees to hold second—or third—

[4] From "Where Chronic Inflation Brings Bewildering Results," article in *US News & World Report*. 77:55-6. S. 2, '74.

jobs elsewhere to earn enough money to cope with rising living costs.

☐ In Brazil, there is worry that the end of huge government subsidies to growers will boost coffee prices. In that case, people in the world's greatest coffee-producing land would no longer be able to afford one of their most enjoyable traditions—frequent coffee breaks during the workday.

☐ Working-class neighborhoods in Chile's urban areas are pockmarked with empty houses. Many field hands who had come to Santiago and other cities in search of the good life are going back to farms and ranches in the belief that food in the countryside is less expensive than in the cities.

A 150-Year Battle

Since Latin American countries won independence from Spain and Portugal a century and a half ago, emperors, elected presidents and military dictators have attacked inflation in a variety of ways. Yet no government has ever found a successful, long-lasting remedy.

Some national currencies were revalued by the simple expedient of lopping two or three zeros off the face value of bank notes and price tags.

For instance, when Brazil gained independence from Portugal in 1822, the currency was the real, said to have been worth about the same as the US dollar of that day.

But as prices continued to soar over the years, the real gave way to the milreis, next to the cruzeiro and then, in 1967, to the "new" cruzeiro.

Today, it would take 7 billion reals—if they were still in use in their original denominations—to equal one US dollar, despite a sharp decline in the purchasing power of the dollar over the same period of time.

Financial authorities say that there are two principal reasons for eliminating the zeros from money—for example, turning a 1,000-cruzeiro banknote into a single cruzeiro:

Cash registers and calculating machines—and customers—

cannot handle money units that range into the thousands or millions for ordinary transactions. When a shirt costs 15,000 pesos, a carton of milk 1,600 and a daily newspaper 350, day-to-day shopping becomes an exercise in higher mathematics for seller and buyer.

When Latin Americans are forced to deal in currencies with inflated face values, they begin to scorn thrift and accuracy. Their attitude: "The money isn't worth anything, anyway."

Imported Trouble

In recent months, most South American governments and businessmen have had to deal with the damage done to national economies by what financial experts term "imported inflation"—arising from the higher cost of goods and materials that must be purchased abroad.

According to official forecasts, Brazil was to have registered a substantial surplus in its 1974 balance of trade. Instead, the military officers and civilian technocrats who run the country learned that petroleum imports would cost at least $3 billion . . . [in 1974], compared with $1 billion in 1973. Costs of imported wheat, machinery and raw material for industry also took sizable jumps. The government . . . estimates foreign trade will be $1 billion in the red . . . [in 1974].

The impact is being widely felt. Retail prices, for example, have been rising at a rate of 3 percent a month. A major bank estimates that the purchasing power of the average worker dropped 20 percent during the first five months of 1974.

This is a big setback in Brazil's drive to bring inflation down to manageable levels from the disastrous rate of 140 percent a year that prevailed before the military took power in 1964. Until the energy crisis knocked the props from under the campaign, inflation had been slashed to below 20 percent a year.

How a "Miracle" Works

The fact that Brazilian authorities had managed to bring prices under partial control—while doubling per capita income and stimulating billions of dollars in domestic and foreign investments—set foreign economists to talking about a "Brazilian miracle."

Experts began arriving from overseas to study how Brazil did it. They found the government using a technique known as "monetary correction" in Brazil and as "indexing" in the US and Europe. Under the system, the values of just about every financial service and many types of contracts, even tax rates, are adjusted at frequent intervals to take into account inflationary changes that have occurred since the previous "correction." Minimum-wage levels are raised once a year.

Financial experts in Brazil do not contend that indexing eliminates inflation—or that it would work efficiently in the US. They do say it takes much of the profit out of speculation in commodities and money, while increases in the cost of living are spread more evenly among the people.

Brazilian government officials and businessmen, although unhappy over the 1974 rate of inflation, are not completely discouraged. They hope that President Ernesto Geisel will be able to prevent inflation from running wild as it did a decade ago.

Woe in a Small Country

If Brazil, South America's largest country, is having difficulty controlling inflation, Uruguay, the continent's smallest nation, is in even more serious trouble.

Uruguay's rate of inflation rose from 77.5 percent in 1972 to 94.7 percent . . . [in 1973] as new pressures from the high cost of energy piled on top of those created by years of a wage-price spiral. . . . [The 1974] rate is expected to be about 2 percent a week.

"Balance sheets mean little, profits mean little," complains a business executive in Montevideo. "You can show a whopping big profit, which the government taxes, but when you try to replace your stock, you find that you actually lost money."

To a factory employee, inflation means taking a second job—as a taxi driver, for instance—to earn a living wage.

To a university physics professor, inflation means working as an electrician and appliance repairman to make ends meet. To a company owner, it means finding some way to skirt government wage ceilings in order to meet the needs of his employees.

Companies or individuals with bank checking accounts must be doubly careful because the government has outlawed overdrafts.

A Uruguayan bank which honors a check for which there is insufficient funds will be fined. The person who wrote the check will have his account closed and his name will be publicized in the newspapers.

The Uruguayan government has adopted Brazil's system of small, frequent devaluations of the currency and has imposed price and wage controls. Wages went up an average of 17 percent in June.

But prices jumped, too. Milk rose 38 percent, rice 9 percent, flour 20 percent and cheese 30 percent.

Exit the Middle Class

"The middle class is catching it in the neck, as usual," says a foreign diplomat. "They're cutting back on expenses, selling off personal possessions, leaving the country. It's really heart-rending."

A European banker in Montevideo sums up the situation this way: "Uruguayans have been living with inflation for years, and they still don't know how to deal with it."

It is much the same story in Argentina. According to official statistics, retail prices rose 15.1 percent during the first half of 1974. Other nongovernmental experts insist the increase actually ranges between 20 and 32 percent and predict inflation for the full year could be as high as 50 percent.

How does an Argentine worker combat inflation? "Get another job and go into debt," a white-collar worker in Buenos Aires explains. "This is traditional in Argentina."

Argentines, a banker comments, are reluctant to accept a lower standard of living and do everything possible to increase their income.

"People gamble more now," he says. "Pari-mutuel receipts at Argentine race tracks are running at record levels. A man figures, 'My 1,000 pesos aren't going to last me until the end of the month anyway. So I might as well try to run them up to 2,000 or so.' "

Learning to Cope

An Argentine bookkeeper, determined to protect himself against the long-range effects of inflation, is putting his spare cash into "capital goods," rather than allowing inflation to eat into a savings account. He is making payments on an apartment and a car, and has purchased several pieces of gold jewelry in belief their value in real terms will appreciate.

The bookkeeper, like most South Americans, is convinced that inflation is here to stay.

His day-to-day existence, therefore, centers on learning to cope with inflation, not with outlasting it.

"There is a sense of perpetually running in place," he says. "But what else is there for us to do?"

THE GREEN GIANT AND THE HEMISPHERE [5]

For the present, Brazil's approach to the rest of the world is like Japan's: guided mainly by commercial priori-

[5] From "Brazil," Fact Sheet no 3. In *Great Decisions 1975*. Foreign Policy Association. '75. p 33-5. Reprinted by permission. Copyright, 1975 by Foreign Policy Association, Inc. 345 E. 46th St. New York 10017.

ties. Brazil's main worries are that its export sales may be restricted by protectionist barriers in the industrialized countries and the limited purchasing power of the developing countries, and that Brazilian imports of oil and other vital necessities may be curtailed by international shortages and inflated prices.

Thus the Brazilians are eager to wrap up a new trade agreement with their biggest regional market, the nine-nation European Economic Community, which now absorbs a third of all Brazilian exports. They are pressing the US, which absorbs about a quarter, to lower its tariffs on manufactured and processed goods from developing countries. They are cultivating Japan as a key customer for Brazilian soybeans, sugar and other commodities. Nor does their ideological hatred of communism deter them from doing business with Communist countries (except Cuba). Brazil is selling sugar to China, buying coal from Poland and developing a diversified two-way trade with the Soviet Union; 130 Brazilian companies recently displayed their wares for Soviet buyers at a commercial exhibit in Moscow.

Africa is another commercial target. The Brazilians have been courting independent black Africa with an eye on its mineral treasure: copper from Zaïre, oil from Nigeria, etc. Oil hunger is also drawing them into closer relations with the Arab world. Braspetro, the international operations subsidiary of Petrobrás, is busily pursuing joint oil exploration deals with Egypt, Iraq and other Middle East producers.

But the main thrust of Brazil's oil hunt and export drive is much closer to home: the South American continent.

Sphere of Influence

The Brazilians see valuable growth potential for their industrial exports and convenient access to energy imports in the neighboring Spanish-speaking states. There is just one cloud on the horizon. Six neighbors—Venezuela, Colombia, Ecuador, Peru, Chile and Bolivia—have banded together in a budding common market known as the Andean

Group. Even if no additional neighbors join, the Brazilians worry about being shut out of a trading "bloc" of 73 million consumers. So they have launched a multipronged offensive —diplomacy, direct investment, commercial credit, outright development aid—to lure the surrounding countries into Brazil's economic orbit.

Three small countries on Brazil's borders are already its virtual satellites. In Bolivia (5 million people), the poorest nation on the continent, the Brazilians are helping to build a steel industry that will utilize Bolivia's iron ore reserves and a pipeline that will pump its natural gas into Brazil. In Paraguay (2.7 million population) they are pouring investments into cattle ranching and other enterprises. The most ambitious "joint" venture, however, is a giant hydroelectric dam to be built at Itaipu, where the Paraná River forms the border between Paraguay and Brazil. With a projected capacity of 10.7 million kilowatts, Itaipu will be the biggest hydropower station in the world. Agrarian Paraguay will have minimal need for the electricity produced and will sell most of its share to Brazil for $30 million a year. Uruguay (3 million people) has traditionally lain within Argentina's orbit, but now it is sometimes jokingly called "Brazil's twenty-third state." Its huge northern neighbor has moved in with generous credits and military aid—Uruguay's military masters, like Bolivia's and Paraguay's, are politically congenial to Brazil's conservative generals—and Brazilian investors have been greedily buying up Uruguayan ranches and urban real estate.

Brazil's biggest, richest and most powerful neighbor, Argentina, is a different case. Historically the two countries have always been rivals. Although they have never gone to war, the Brazilians have kept half of their army permanently stationed in the south to guard against a possible invasion by the Argentines. (Proportionately, the latter are more heavily militarized: Argentina's population is one quarter the size of Brazil's but its well-equipped military forces are nearly two thirds as large.) Today, however, Brazil's leaders feel more confident. They see Argentina's political influence diminished by decades of instability and its status as an industrial competitor weakened by years of inflation. Relations between the two countries now appear reasonably good—if less "equal." The main bone of contention is the Itaipu hydroelectric project. The Argentines have protested —so far in vain—that a huge dam and artificial lake on one of the key tributaries of the Plata basin could have disastrous effects further downstream, on fishing, navigation, irrigation and even the Buenos Aires water supply.

Further north, the Brazilians are eagerly seeking to expand their influence. This is where the oil is: in the Amazon jungles on the eastern flank of the Andes and in the Maracaibo and Orinoco basins of Venezuela. Early last year the first oil shipments from Peru's newly opened fields started the long journey by river barge to Manaus on the Brazilian Amazon. In Colombia, Braspetro is half owner of an exploration venture expected to yield 100 million barrels of oil and is building its first refinery outside of Brazil. Joint oil and gas deals with Ecuador are also on the agenda and Brazilians are pursuing new accords with Venezuela. Other Brazilian investments are in the works: Colombian coal, Peruvian metals, a highway that will link Manaus with the Venezuelan capital, Caracas.

"Imperialist" Ambitions?

Brazil's territorial borders with Venezuela, Colombia and Peru are largely uninhabited jungle with ill-defined frontier lines. But now Brazilians are starting to penetrate these remote areas to settle in and look for oil of their own. And their northwestern neighbors are becoming nervous about Brazilian territorial "encroachment." It is only one symptom of a wider apprehension among South Americans. The green giant is rising to his full height, feeling his new strength and beginning to take strides toward his "manifest destiny." Is that destiny to be imperial hegemony? Is Brazil's ambition to dominate the southern continent?

A common view on the Left of the Latin American spectrum holds that Washington's lessened interest and lowered profile in Latin America have created a power vacuum there. And Brasília, with Washington's blessing, is moving in to fill it. The US "has anointed Brazil as its anti-Communist watchdog and capitalist showcase for South America," writes a commentator in Lima. . . .

The Brazilians scoff at this image of themselves as "surrogate Yankees." They label it plain jealousy, nothing more, on the part of Latin Americans who are frustrated by domestic failures and seeking a new external scapegoat to replace the receding US presence. The envy is a backhanded tribute to Brazil's success. . . . Economic influence, certainly this can only benefit Brazil's more "backward" neighbors. But territorial intervention, certainly not. "Why should we want to go that far?" protests another diplomat. "There is so much territory left to conquer within our own frontiers."

Washington, for its part, categorically denies having appointed Brazil its "agent" for the southern hemisphere. . . .

The View From the North

What most concerns the US today is its commercial interests in Brazil—specifically, the weakening of the American competitive position in the worldwide scramble for Brazilian business. "We are now in a world of buyers and sellers, not 'donors and recipients,'" emphasizes a former World Bank official. . . . Item: In competitive bidding to supply $200 million worth of steelmaking machinery to Brazil, Americans came in fourth after the Japanese, the West Germans and the Italians. Item: In the five years from 1966 to 1971 the *share* of Brazil's imports supplied by the US fell from 40 percent to 29 percent (even though the gross *volume* of American sales increased).

Brazil ranks second only to Mexico as a Latin American market for US exports, accounting for more than one fifth of our total sales to the region. Our businessmen, understandably, are eager to see that market grow along with Brazil's booming economy. But can they hold their own—in selling price, credit terms, product quality, delivery, service—against the competition? "There is something almost pathetic," commented a US consular official in Rio to an editor of the Foreign Policy Association, "about all the Americans who come rushing down here hoping for a piece of the action—only to find that some European or Japanese has beaten them to it with a better offer."

The Brazilians are also dependent on the US market, of course. We are still their single biggest customer, taking more than a third of their green coffee exports and about 80 percent of their footwear exports. But the bullish world market for commodities in short supply gives them considerable leverage. At the beginning of 1974, for example, they decided they would export fewer bags of coffee at a higher price per bag—and still be able to take in more cash than they did in 1973.

Another prime concern of US businessmen is their direct investments in Brazil. These now amount to $2.5 billion—15 percent of total US investment in the Western Hemisphere outside of Canada. In the longer run, however, the Brazilians' hospitality to the multinational corporations cannot be taken for granted. Will they decide one day to join the prevailing Latin American trend, proclaim their economic independence and dispense with the capital of foreign investors?

One US contribution is already being phased out: bilateral development loans. In the 1963-73 decade Brazil received $3.2 billion in official aid and credits from Washington. By 1974 it was allotted only $17 million, a two-thirds reduction from the preceding year, and no new programs are scheduled for 1975. Brazil continues to get generous loans from multilateral agencies such as the Inter-American Development Bank and the World Bank; in fact, it is the latter institution's single biggest borrower.

Although few Americans quarrel with the end of our bilateral aid to Brazil, other aspects of US policy toward that country have come under criticism. Is it morally right for Washington to bestow its friendship and respect so openly on a regime that tortures political prisoners? Testifying to a congressional committee about the reports of Brazilian atrocities, a State Department official noted that "while we have made our concern clear to the government of Brazil, we have sought to avoid direct public intervention." Is this carrying Washington's pragmatic policy of non-intervention a bit too far?

In 1973 the Administration broke with previous American policy and authorized the sale of supersonic jet fighter planes to five South American countries, including Brazil. For American aircraft manufacturers, the decision means some valuable export business that would otherwise go to their competitors in Europe. But do the American people want to buttress the power of the Brazilian military rulers with sophisticated military hardware? Are we helping to prolong the reign of the generals—and perhaps supporting some dangerous great-power ambitions they may develop in the future?

"First World" or "Third World"?

So far, Brazil has defined its future ambitions only in vague terms. . . . [A former Brazilian president] once sketched his country's international horizons as a series of concentric circles: First, Brazil's immediate neighbors in Latin America. Next, the entire Western Hemisphere including the US and Canada. Then, a choice of alternatives: either equal membership in the broad Western community of industrialized non-Communist nations (the First World), or leadership of the developing nations (the Third World). And finally, the global community as a whole.

A number of observers feel that the moment of choice between a First- and Third-World role for Brazil is fast approaching, and that we should help guide the choice toward the first alternative. We can, for example, invite Brazil to join the twenty-three-member Organization for Economic

Cooperation and Development. If the Greeks, the Turks, the Spaniards and the Portuguese can belong to this "rich man's club," does it make sense to exclude the Brazilians?

Unless the highly nationalistic Brazilians are welcomed into the larger fold of mature Western nations, caution these analysts, their diplomatic isolation could provoke new tensions between the First and Third worlds. We could be confronted with an unruly and unpredictable green giant, flexing its muscles and testing its power among its smaller Latin American neighbors—and even against the US. The day might come, as one commentator has warned, "when the colossus of the north finds itself eyeball-to-eyeball with the colossus of the south."

CREDIT FOR DEVELOPMENT [6]

Argentina

Since Argentina joined the World Bank in 1956, the World Bank's activity in the country has been directed toward the development of electric power and transport and, to a small extent, agriculture. The International Finance Corporation has given support to the industrial sector through commitments with several private companies. Nine loans for a total of $532.3 million and nine IFC [International Finance Corporation] investments totaling $39.21 million represent the World Bank Group's financial support to Argentina's development effort. [The World Bank Group consists of the World Bank itself, which lends money for development projects at commercial interest rates; the International Development Association, which makes low-interest loans; and the IFC, referred to above.—Ed.]

Although no Bank loans have been made to Argentina recently, the Argentine government and the Bank have been working together on project preparation and supervision

    [6] From *The World Bank Group in the Americas*. International Bank for Reconstruction and Development (World Bank). 1818 H St. N.W. Washington, D.C. 20433. Excerpts reprinted by permission.

of on-going projects supported by earlier loans. In the future, the emphasis in Bank operations in Argentina may shift to the development of agriculture and industry.

Agriculture. The Argentine agricultural sector employs only one fifth of the country's labor force but generates about 85 percent of its exports. Within the sector, cattle raising ranks as high as farming. Three fourths of the country's agricultural production comes from the pampas, a fertile crescent lying within a four-hundred-mile radius around Buenos Aires.

In July 1967, the Bank made a loan of $15.3 million in support of the Argentine government's efforts to expand and modernize the cattle industry. Meat and meat products are extremely important to the economy; beef production alone normally accounts for about one third of Argentina's annual export earnings. The purpose of the program which the Bank is helping to finance is to demonstrate that increased ranch production is technically feasible and financially rewarding. It involves raising beef production by increasing the cattle-carrying capacity of the land through improved pasture and herd management, rather than expanding the acreage under pasture. About 544,000 acres will be improved on approximately 700 ranches located in the pampas. This project was prepared with the assistance of the Food and Agriculture Organization of the United Nations (FAO) under a Cooperative Program with the Bank where the two institutions work together in identifying and preparing projects.

Electric Power. The electric power sector has been the chief recipient of Bank funds. By December 31, 1973, the Bank had made four loans for that sector totaling $292 million.

The Bank's lending for electric power has been the result of an extensive study of the country's needs carried out in 1959-60. One of the principal conclusions of that study was that the greatest need for power was in the Buenos Aires metropolitan area. The Bank's assistance therefore has been aimed at increasing the supply and distribution of electricity in that region, channeling the bulk of the Bank financing to Servicios Eléctricos del Gran Buenos Aires (SEGBA). This is an agency responsible for providing electric power to the metropolitan area. SEGBA has received three loans for a total of $210 million.

The first one, of $95 million made in 1962, helped SEGBA to complete a ... thermal plant, to construct a high-tension interconnection network and to expand the company's distribution system. Two more loans, one of $55 million made in 1968, and another of $60 million made in 1969 have supported SEGBA's expansion program to improve its services.

The fourth Bank loan for power in Argentina, of $82 million, was made in 1968 to Hidroeléctrica Nor Patagónica (Hidronor) to help finance the first stage of Argentina's large hydroelectric scheme, the El Chocón-Cerros Colorados, in northern Patagonia. The first units of the ... complex are already in operation. ...

Industry. The World Bank Group support to Argentina's industrial development has been extended through the International Finance Corporation (IFC) which by December 31, 1973 had made nine commitments for a total of $39.21 million.

The most recent IFC investment consisted in a loan of $10 million to help finance a $72.5 million expansion project of Celulosa Argentina S.A., the largest pulp and paper producer in Argentina, and one of the three largest in Latin America. The project is to expand pulp production capacity from 145,000 tons to 245,000 tons per year, and paper production capacity from 188,000 tons to 292,000 tons per year. The expansion will enable the company to increase the production of several types of printing and writing paper, kraft papers, special wrapping papers, corrugated containers and boxboards, fiber pulps, and caustic soda and chlorine. IFC has also made investments in other Argentine pulp and paper companies and in steel products, automotive parts, petrochemical products and cement companies.

Transportation. Three loans for highway improvement programs and one loan for a railroad reorganization and rehabilitation program have been the World Bank's financial contribution to the Argentine transport sector since 1961, when the first highway loan was approved.

These loans have assisted the government through the years in improving the capacity and efficiency of the nation's transportation system in support of the growth of the economy. The main objective has been to assure a reliable intermodal balance and the most efficient use of resources through better coordination and sound investment planning. The Bank's transportation lending was initially based on the recommendations of a planning group which was organized in 1960 to survey the long-term requirements of Argentina's transportation services.

The transportation study as well as the study of the power sector were partially financed by the UNDP [United Nations Development Program], with the Bank acting as executing agency.

Highways: The three loans to Argentina were for $48.5 million in 1961, made when the planning group's study was not yet completed; $25 million in 1969, and $67.5 million in 1971.

The first loan supported a varied program that included rehabilitation of some 1,600 miles of roads divided into relatively short sections, in such widely distant parts of the country as Patagonia and the subtropical north; due to initial delays, some sections had to be eliminated from the project, and as a result $17.5 million of the original loan was canceled. The second loan helped finance improvement of some 500 miles in four sections of primary roads, and the implementation of measures expected to lead to proper planning in the future development of the highway sector. The third and most recent highway loan is assisting construction or improvement of about 700 miles of roads in different regions of the country; part of the loan's funds were allocated to a feasibility and engineering study of an additional 2,200 miles of highways.

Railways: After the adoption by the government of a comprehensive program of rehabilitation and modernization of the country's railways system, the Bank made in 1971 a loan of $84 million to Ferrocarriles Argentinos, the autonomous corporate organization responsible for the subsector.

Proceeds of the Bank loan include funds for purchasing freight cars, rehabilitating locomotives and cars, renewing and maintaining track, and procuring telecommunication equipment.

Colombia

Cooperation between the government of Colombia and the World Bank has been centered in the basic sectors of the country's infrastructure in support of specific economic development objectives. In transportation (roads and railways), power and telecommunications, for example, an objective has been to link formerly isolated geographic regions of the country and to provide the basis for industrial growth and interregional and foreign trade. Bank Group assistance for industry and agriculture aimed, among other things, at increasing nontraditional exports so that Colombia could reduce its dependence on coffee.

In the social sectors, the World Bank has supported the expansion of the water-supply services for Colombia's growing urban population. Since 1968, the Bank has also been engaged in helping an on-going program to restructure the country's secondary education system to help overcome a serious shortage of middle-level manpower in the urban and rural areas.

Bank Group assistance for Colombia's economic development has not been limited to lending. In June 1949, before the first loan was made, the Bank, at the request of the Colombian government, sent a mission to Colombia to assist in the preparation of a national development program. Colombia was the first member country [of the World Bank Group] to receive this type of assistance. That mission was followed by others which have assisted the government in subsequent years in formulating development programs. Throughout the years the Bank has provided a wide variety of technical assistance.

Through its loans the Bank has cooperated in institution building, mobilization of domestic resources, and improvement of broad economic and sector policies. Also, in 1963 the Bank organized a consultative group to coordinate external assistance to Colombia. This was the first group of its kind established for a member country, and it has since served as a model for those of a number of other nations in different parts of the world. These efforts of the Bank have resulted in an increase in the number and amount of loans to Colombia from the Bank and other lenders. Colombia now ranks fourth among the World Bank's ninety borrowing countries, and third among the borrowing countries in Latin America.

Agriculture. Colombia has maintained a satisfactory agricultural growth rate in recent years. However, a 3.3 percent yearly increase in population and an uneven land distribution continue to contribute to rural poverty, an exodus toward the cities, and urban unemployment.

The Bank financial assistance to the Colombian agricultural sector has aimed at supporting efforts to overcome those problems, to contribute to the growth of the country's nontraditional exports, and to promote modernization of agriculture. The Bank loans have helped finance projects of land reform and land settlement, irrigation, livestock development, and agricultural credit. In all, there have been eight loans totaling $84.1 million for agricultural development....

Education. The Colombian government is implementing a restructuring of its secondary education system to meet the country's increasing needs for trained middle-level manpower. The Bank has assisted this program with three loans, in 1968, 1970 and 1973 totaling $35.3 million. The main thrust of the Bank lending has been to support the creation of comprehensive, technically-oriented secondary schools with a view to preparing students both for the labor market and for further studies, and accelerating the shift in enrollment from academic to industrial and agricultural studies.

The first two Bank loans, of $7.6 million and $6.5 million helped to construct and equip 19 diversified secondary schools located in large urban centers serving nearly 80,000 students on a double shift basis.

The third loan, $21.2 million approved in mid-1973, is helping a project designed to reinforce the on-going program. The project includes the construction and equipping in the next four years of 24 common facilities centers to serve 109,000 students, and of 13 rural comprehensive secondary schools enrolling 7,000 new students and providing for 1,700 boarding places. The 24 centers will provide workshops and laboratories to enable 91 existing secondary schools to diversify their curriculum combining practical and academic subjects. The rural schools will open up opportunities for lower secondary education now lacking in Colombia's rural areas. These schools are expected to provide the basis for an education extension service to support rural development, and will become part of a government program to establish 39 similar schools throughout the country. Under the project, approximately 2,000 teachers will be trained in industrial and other practical subjects over the period 1974-77, to provide technical teachers for the centers and rural schools. . . .

In addition, a survey will be made to evaluate the past development of the education system and to plan for future development. Studies will also be carried out on manpower needs, experience in the introduction of diversified secondary education, and local production of educational equipment and learning materials. Institutional improvements in education administration and planning will be supported by concurrent United Nations Development Program technical assistance.

Telecommunications. In 1967 the World Bank approved a $16 million loan to help finance the 1967-70 program for improvement and expansion by the Empresa Nacional de Telecomunicaciones (TELECOM) of Colombia. Because the existing system was inadequate for the volume of traffic, the program gave priority to improving long distance telephone service.

In 1971 the Bank made a second loan, amounting to $15 million, to TELECOM. The project comprises about 80 percent of TELECOM's 1971-74 expansion program. Among its many components which include new microwave links, . . . [high frequency] routes, increased telex lines and teleprinters in Bogotá, the project involves the installation of 42,000 lines of local exchange equipment of which 18,000 will be for 200 small towns, with a total population of 2 million, presently lacking telephone service.

Transportation. Massive investment in surface transportation has been required in Colombia to overcome the difficult nature of the country's topography. The Bank Group has cooperated with the Colombian government to overcome this obstacle, focusing on two basic aspects: modernization of the railroads and the construction and maintenance of about 2,000 miles of roads. Bank loans and IDA credits for both these purposes total over $250 million.

Water Supply. Most of the water supply and sewerage systems in Colombia have lagged behind the rapid growth of the urban populations. Because of a large and steady migration from rural areas, particularly to the largest urban centers, the number of urban inhabitants as a percentage of the country's population increased from less than 40 percent in 1960 to 57 percent in 1970.

The inability of most muncipalities to mobilize local resources has prevented them from providing adequate water and sewerage services to the urban population. As part of the government's policy in this area, measures are being taken to mobilize additional resources through adequate tariffs. Although the sector has grown relatively rapidly during the past six years, it is estimated that about one fourth of the urban population still lacks direct access to water supply and sewerage services.

In 1972, the Bank made a loan of $9.1 million to help overcome the serious deficiency in water supply and sewerage in seven cities with populations between 80,000 and 300,000. . . . Of the seven cities included in the project, the borrowing utility companies in five are responsible not only for water supply but also for other public services such as power, telecommunications and slaughterhouses. The improved services will be provided in areas mainly inhabited by lower-income groups. The purpose of the project is to insure that some 1.6 million people, or double the population being supplied now, will be served with an adequate supply of wholesome water. The seven-city project will also substantially improve sanitary conditions, and help to reduce pollution of streams.

IV. CHILE IN TURMOIL

EDITOR'S INTRODUCTION

In 1970, Salvador Allende came to power by winning a plurality of votes cast in the Chilean election that year. He thus became the world's first Marxist to become president in a country where voters had a choice among several competing political parties and ideologies. Allende also was a man committed to democracy. Although many thought Marxism and democracy were incompatible goals, Allende set out to prove them wrong. However, because of Allende's policies, including expropriation of big foreign-owned industries, the economy quickly ran into serious trouble and opposition mounted throughout the country.

The end came with stunning suddenness. The armed forces of Chile led a revolt that overthrew the government, with Allende himself either being killed or committing suicide in the presidential palace just as it was being stormed by the rebels. The victorious armed forces immediately rounded up thousands of his supporters, executing some and jailing many.

The articles in this section trace the fall of the Allende regime and note what has happened in Chile since that time. The first tells the story of the Allende years through 1972 and shows how the economic problems of the country were racing out of control, thus setting the stage for the coup which eventually occurred. Inflation was growing, production falling, and dissatisfaction spreading.

The second article carries the story through much of 1973 and outlines what actually happened during the days of the bloody revolution that resulted in Allende's death and the overthrow of his regime. The concluding report picks up the story after the revolution and describes how the new regime has effectively silenced opposition and dissent of every kind.

PROBLEMS IN ALLENDE'S CHILE [1]

October and November, 1972, saw Chile's President Salvador Allende Gossens facing his most severe crisis . . . [with] many sectors of the commercial and professional middle class . . . on strike. A proposal to nationalize transport services in Chile's far south produced a nationwide strike of 40,000 . . . [truck] owners and drivers, supported by small shopkeepers, engineers, doctors and other professional groups. The strike is estimated to have cost Chile something between $100 million and $150 million. Twenty provinces were placed under a state of emergency, and a midnight curfew was declared.

Allende's response to this challenge was to involve the military much more heavily in the governing of the country, though not without opposition from the left of his own Socialist party and from the Movement of the Revolutionary Left (MIR). . . .

The most important economic indicator in Chilean politics is the rate of inflation. In the first nine months of 1971, Allende's government had reduced it to a respectable 14 percent; but in the first nine months of 1972 the rate had leapt to 100 percent. By the end of 1972, it . . . [was] nearer 140 percent 150 percent, a record for a country where inflation has been endemic. The government, in line with its aim of defending the interest of the working class, brought forward by three months the usual readjustment of wage levels to take account of inflation, and in October declared a wage increase equivalent to the increase in the cost of living. . . .

No one doubts the seriousness of the present situation. Allende himself has declared that the economy is on a war footing. It is not difficult to produce the figures which un-

[1] From article by Alan Angell, university lecturer and fellow, St. Anthony's College, Oxford. *Current History.* 64:57-60+. F. '73. Reprinted by permission.

derline the gravity of the present situation, in contrast to the rather encouraging economic performance of 1971. The gross national product rose by 7 percent–8 percent in 1971, partly because very considerable unused industrial capacity was brought into production following increased demand as Allende's government substantially improved the real wages of the working class. All the signs are, however, that the rise in 1972 is likely to be only half that of the previous year— industrial production, which rose by 14 percent in 1971, registered a much smaller increase in 1972. The boom in the construction industry in 1971 has slackened as the building program of the public sector has declined.

The failure of the economy to respond to increased demand is most clearly marked in the agricultural sector. In 1971, Chile exported $7 million less in foodstuff than in 1970, but imported $136 million more. The total import bill for food in 1972 is likely to rise to a colossal $400 million, not far short of the likely deficit in the balance of payments. To put it another way, 35 percent of the import capacity of Chile goes for foodstuff that could be produced locally. Yet these figures overstate the economic mismanagement of the government, for Chile is also the victim of the high price of food, especially beef and wheat, on the world market. A great deal of the rise in the import bill is absorbed in higher prices, not in extra quantities of imports. Chile has suffered similar misfortunes in respect to copper prices. In 1969, the world price of copper was 69 cents per pound; in 1971, it was only 49 cents per pound. So although production of the large mines went up by 7 percent in 1971 over 1970 (when production had fallen over 1969 because of initial difficulties involved in the nationalization process), Chile's foreign earnings were sharply curtailed. The previous balance of payments surplus of the Christian Democratic government was due to high copper prices, not better economic management.

The impact of high food prices and low copper prices shows up in the balance of payments figures. A surplus of $91 million in 1970 became a deficit of $311 million in 1971.

And the export figures for the first six months of 1972 show a 20 percent fall over the 1971 levels. These figures acquire sinister potency in the light of Chile's enormous foreign indebtedness—once again a legacy of previous governments and not the product of the policy of the . . . government. Chile faced repayments of $1,400 million in the six-year period of Allende's presidency. Faced with the hostility of the United States Government, and backed only by slender international reserves of $30 million, Allende's economic team pulled off something like a diplomatic coup in persuading the group of international creditors known as the Club of Paris to renegotiate part of that debt repayment. Yet for 1972 there still remains $490 million in amortization and interest repayments. Soviet credits have been forthcoming. In 1971, Chile received the equivalent of $97 million (repayable over ten years at 3 percent interest); and in 1972 so far there have been short-term credits of $50 million in hard currencies as well as other credits tied to Soviet products.

But that still leaves an enormous gap. The problem has been intensified by the hostile action of the Kennecott Copper Corporation, still determined to get compensation for its assets nationalized by the government. Because of a challenge to the right of the government to sell copper in Europe, the French judiciary has been brought into the debate on the ownership of a shipload of copper recently delivered to France. Whatever the outcome, the affair has increased the state of anxiety prevailing about the Chilean economy and, more seriously, has held up several important credits allocated to Chile by international agencies. [The current Chilean government has since discussed payment to Kennecott.—Ed.]

Economic Solutions?

Clearly, Allende's long-term economic strategy is in jeopardy unless he can devise some solutions to the short-term problems. But it is difficult to see what he can do. Take the balance of payments problem, for example. He might try to obtain more short-term credits, but this is difficult, given the hostility of the US, and would increase the problem, already enormous, of future repayment. Defaulting on repayments has been advocated on the extreme Left, but Chile still needs credits and markets outside the Soviet bloc. Perhaps imports could be severely restricted, but this is not likely to increase the government's popularity when it needs all the support it can muster for the forthcoming elections. Allende must be praying that the world price of copper will rise to the dizzy heights it did under [his predecessor] Eduardo Frei Montalvo's Christian Democratic government.

The pressing problem for the government is how to contain the rate of inflation, and how to increase the rate of investment. In 1971, one area which showed signs of future trouble was the absence of any new investment outside the construction sector. It is easy to see why the private sector is reluctant to invest, given the policy of expropriation and nationalization undertaken by the government. The state has had its problems in this area too. Chile is the first country to elect a Marxist president. One of the decisive factors in that election was the support given to him by the organized working class. And the unions expect their payoff. The government has found it difficult to persuade unionists when they have taken over a factory that the profits do not all go to the members. . . .

Though the stage was set for inflation in 1971—in that year the quantity of money in circulation increased by 120 percent—the actual rate of inflation was modest, compared with what was to come. Unemployment, considerable reserves in the economy, and unused capacity allowed for an increase in supply adequate to meet the demand created by large wage increases. But if consumer demand was satisfied, the requirements of long-term economic growth were not, and in 1972 the consequences of these inflationary pressures were fully felt.

One possible solution . . . would be to limit the prices

of essential goods consumed by the working class, and there already exist state agencies . . . for this purpose. But the process of state control has not yet advanced far enough to make that sort of policy practicable. The government would need to control the commercial life of the country much more tightly before it could be sure of effectively limiting price rises, eliminating the black market, and ensuring an equitable process of distribution. The strike of the . . . [truck] owners, most of whom own only a vehicle or two, indicates the extent of resistance to the policies of the . . . government not just at the level of large industrialists but also at the level of petty bourgeois concerns. As Allende's electoral strategy is partly aimed at separating the petty bourgeoisie from the entrepreneurial and large commercial sector, any policies that threaten the livelihood of small businessmen are likely to have damaging political consequences.

Economic Achievements

This picture of unrelieved economic gloom should not hide the real changes brought about by the Allende government. The danger is that short-term problems threaten to overwhelm the government.

When Allende took power two years ago, the economy was largely dominated by monopolistic industrial enterprises, with substantial sectors under the control of American interests, and with the state aiding and reinforcing that economic structure. It is true that the Frei administration effected considerable changes, but on a much smaller scale than those of the present government.

Direct control of the public sector over industrial production has risen from 10 percent in 1970 to 30 percent in 1971 and to over 40 percent in 1972. Given the fact that 22 percent of value added in manufacturing comes from small and artisanal enterprises, the government can well claim to control the commanding heights of the economy. The state now controls 85 percent of exports and 45 percent of imports. Private banks, American copper companies, steel, cement, coal—all these vital areas now belong to what is called by the government the "social area" of the economy. If the transition to socialism depends on state control over the industrial and financial structure, then that foundation has been securely laid.

The agrarian sector has seen similar transformation, although here admittedly the process of reform was well advanced under the Frei government, and the growth of rural unions took place under the guidance of the Christian Democrats—thanks to the law that they passed in 1967. Most estates of over 80 hectares—the size laid down by the law—have been incorporated into the agrarian reform sector. Up to 1970, 1,400 estates were taken over and since then another 3,160, comprising in total nearly 54 percent of the agricultural land (excluding the far south). However, the process of creating the so-called Agrarian Reform Centers to run the expropriated estates is a much more laborious and complicated procedure, fraught with political difficulties, and the process of agrarian reform is thus far from complete.

The major beneficiary of the first reforms of Allende was of course the working class. Unemployment was reduced from 8.3 percent in 1970 to 3.8 percent in 1971, though it has risen slightly since then. The share of wages and salaries in the national income rose from 53 percent in 1970 to 59 percent in 1971. Participation in the running of enterprises has not risen so sharply, however, and the left of Allende's coalition would like to see a much more rapid process of mobilization and integration of the working class into controlled economic activity. But Allende has always preferred to proceed cautiously in this area, especially as the Christian Democrats are still in a strong position in the union movement—they obtained about a quarter of the votes in the recent national union elections, and are probably the largest single union group in Santiago. Decentralization could mean, in some places, handing over control to the opposition.

THE BLOODY END OF A MARXIST DREAM [2]

For two terrible days [in September 1973], the capital of Chile turned into a bloody battleground. Planes roared in almost at rooftop level, firing rockets and sowing bombs. Tanks rumbled through the streets, tearing holes in walls with shells from their cannon. Infantrymen popped up in doorways, and the sound of their fire reverberated through the city. The principal target, the presidential palace, disappeared behind a veil of smoke and flames. Inside, Chile's Marxist President Salvador Allende Gossens, sixy-five, died in his office as a military junta took over his country.

After his inauguration three years ago, Allende had stood on the small balcony outside his office in the palace to launch a great experiment. While thousands of his supporters cheered in the plaza below, he announced a unique undertaking: he intended to lead Chile along a democratic road to socialism. Last week the balcony still stood, although the palace was a smoldering ruin. So was Allende's Marxist vision for his country.

Week after week, as a succession of bitter strikes plunged Chile toward economic chaos, rumors had circulated in Santiago that the country was on the verge of a military coup. Even so, many Chileans dismissed the stories. True, Chile had large and well-trained armed forces. But unlike the colonels of neighboring Peru and the generals of Brazil, Chile's officers had by and large a nonpolitical tradition.

Instant Martyr

Chileans who thought that their country was somehow immune from military takeovers were wrong. Moreover, the coup that ended Allende's experiment in socialism proved to be extraordinarily violent even by Latin American standards. In the flurry of fighting that accompanied the *golpe* (coup) and in the two days of chaos that followed, several

[2] From article in *Time*. 102:35-8+. S. 24, '73. Reprinted by permission from *Time*, the Weekly Newsmagazine; Copyright Time Inc.

thousand people were killed or injured. The military claimed that Allende had killed himself rather than surrender. Allende's supporters insisted that he had been murdered. In a sense, the manner of his death was irrelevant. Almost overnight, he became an instant martyr for leftists the world over—and a legendary specter that may well haunt Latin America for years.

Allende's downfall had implications that reached far beyond the borders of Chile. His had been the first democratically elected Marxist government in Latin America. Moderate Latins will certainly want no more such experiments because of Chile's experience; leftists, on the other hand, will ruefully conclude that revolution is a surer route to power than the ballot box. The US was embarrassed by the coup—though Washington insisted that it had taken no part. Anti-imperialists everywhere immediately assumed that Washington was behind his downfall. At week's end the US had made no move to recognize the new government, but most observers expected an improvement in relations. The change of Chilean governments might also affect US corporations; their sizable holdings had been taken over by Allende, but they now might at least be reimbursed for what they had lost by a more sympathetic government.

The coup was carefully planned and meticulously executed. . . . Armored cars rolled across Santiago's broad Plaza de la Constitución to block the portals of La Moneda, the somber eighteenth-century-style presidential palace. As army sharpshooters took up positions, at least one hundred armed *carabineros*—Chile's paramilitary police—jumped out of buses and double-timed across the square. Their mission, according to the secret order of the day, was "to restore institutional normality" in South America's most democratic nation and "stop a disastrous dictatorship from installing itself."

Allende had apparently heard rumors; at the uncharacteristically early hour of 7:15, he had driven to La Moneda from his comfortable villa in Santiago's Barrio Alto district.

As the troops began to assemble outside the palace, General Augusto Pinochet Ugarte, commander in chief of the army, telephoned an ultimatum to the palace. If Allende surrendered his office, he would be given safe-conduct out of the country; otherwise he would be deposed by force. Allende refused. "I will not resign," he declared in a very brief radio broadcast. "I am prepared to die if necessary." He urged workers—the most loyal and enthusiastic supporters of his socialist program—to seize their factories as a sign of defiance. As Hawker Hunters of the Chilean air force swooped low over the palace, Allende made a final appearance on his second-floor balcony and waved to a small band of curious citizens whom the army had not yet shooed away.

Allende immediately recognized that he faced the worst crisis of his stormy three-year presidency. An hour before the military's ultimatum, he telephoned his wife Hortensia at their villa. "I'm calling from La Moneda," he told her. "The situation has become very grave. The navy has revolted and I am going to stay here." Allende was right. Even before the junta's troops surrounded the palace, the navy had announced that it had taken over and sealed off the port city of Valparaiso, seventy-five miles away. Marines from Valparaiso were advancing on the capital to join the soldiers, airmen and *carabineros* commanded by leaders of the coup.

Allende soon found himself isolated from all potential supporters. A radio station operated by his Socialist party went silent after making a final appeal to enlisted men to disobey the orders of their officers. Another station operated by Allende's Communist partners in the Chilean Unidad Popular (Popular Unity) coalition went dead. Soon the only station left on the air in Santiago was one that identified itself as "the military government radio." Its first order: "The president of the republic must proceed immediately to hand over his high office."

A Mexican journalist . . . , managed to interview fifteen of the people who claim to have last seen Allende alive.

According to his account, the president assembled close friends in the palace and told them: "I will not abandon La Moneda. They will only take me out of here dead." The group included ten members of the security force and thirty youths of a private guard known as el Grupo de Amigos Personales (the Group of Personal Friends).

General Pinochet's call was followed by one from the navy commander, Admiral José Toribio Merino Castro, who repeated the ultimatum. "I will not surrender," Allende declared. "That is a course for cowards like yourself."

As an attack on the palace became imminent, Allende gathered his remnant of supporters in one room of the palace. "Gentlemen," he said, "I am staying." He asked everyone to leave; no one did. Allende then ordered the women to go to the office of the palace major-domo and told the men to take up combat positions. There was a twenty-minute attack by infantry and tanks. During a brief truce, General Pinochet again called the palace, giving Allende fifteen minutes to surrender. Once more the president refused. When the attack halted, the women in the palace—including one of Allende's daughters . . . left for safety.

At noon, a pair of Hawker Hunters attacked the palace with bombs, rockets and tear gas. An hour and a half later, infantrymen entered La Moneda by a side door; their officers gave Allende ten minutes to surrender. "All of you go down without weapons and with hands up," the president told the handful of aides who had stayed with him. "Go and surrender to the army. I will be the last to leave." Then, according to . . . [the Mexican journalist], Allende shot himself.

Mrs. Allende had listened to her husband's final radio broadcast. "At noon, Salvador did not answer the telephone at La Moneda," she said. "When I managed to get through to La Moneda, it was security agents or *carabineros* who answered." Meanwhile the air force was also attacking the house at Barrio Alto. "Between attacks—the planes returned to their base to reload—there was ferocious shooting. The residence was all smoke. The last telephone call I made to

La Moneda, I had to use the telephone lying on the floor."

Not until the next day was Mrs. Allende told that her husband was in a military hospital, wounded. When she went to see him, she learned that he was actually dead. She told newsmen that he had probably killed himself with a submachine gun presented to him by Cuba's Fidel Castro. But rumors spread that Allende had been shot thirteen times —the widow later saw his coffin but never his body—and that he and four aides had been killed in cold blood. The rumors fed the rapidly growing legend of Allende the Marxist martyr.

The same day the body of Allende was trucked to a military airport near Santiago and put aboard a plane bound for the city of Viña del Mar, where the president's family maintained a crypt. Mrs. Allende was allowed to accompany the corpse, as were his sister Laura, two nephews and an aide.

At Santa Inés cemetery, Mrs. Allende, torn between sorrow and fury, picked some flowers and laid them on the coffin. "Salvador Allende cannot be buried in such an anonymous way," she said in a hard voice to the gravediggers. "I want you to know at least the name of the person you are burying."

Meanwhile, the junta moved rapidly to consolidate its rule. In a hasty ceremony at the Bernardo O'Higgins Military School—named in honor of Chile's founding father—a military government that included two right-wing civilians for political window dressing was sworn in. Ominously, the new leaders took an oath of allegiance not to Chile's constitution but to the junta. General Pinochet headed the cabinet as president of the junta. Its other members: Admiral Merino; General Gustavo Leigh Guzmán, air force commander in chief; and General César Mendoza Duran, director general of the *carabineros*. The most important portfolio in the new cabinet—Interior—went to Army General Oscar Bonilla.

The military shut down all of Chile's airports and closed

the borders to Argentina, Bolivia and Peru. A state of siege was imposed throughout the country, and Santiago was subject to a round-the-clock curfew. Violators were warned that they would be shot on sight. While the army struggled to rid Santiago of leftist snipers, householders kept their heads down because itchy soldiers fired whenever a window went up too fast. There were rumors that pro-Allende army units were in command of the southern part of the country. By week's end, the military officially declared that life in the capital was returning to normal. But a stringent curfew remained in effect, the airports stayed closed, and all communications with the outside world were censored.

There were stories that some soldiers had bayoneted prisoners to death without reason, while others, armed with lists of pro-Allende suspects, were making door-to-door searches in Santiago. Anyone found at home was summarily shot. In broadcasts, the names of seventy prominent Socialist and Communist politicians were read off; all those on the list were ordered to surrender at once.

At least one of the wanted men, Socialist party Secretary-General Carlos Altamirano, was said to have been "accidentally" killed during the fighting. There was yet another report that at least three thousand people had been put aboard a prison ship off the coast. Among the alleged internees: Communist poet Pablo Neruda, seventy-nine, winner of the Nobel Prize for Literature in 1971, and Chile's former ambassador to Paris. [Neruda died of cancer in a Santiago hospital on September 23, 1973, only twelve days after the death of his friend President Allende. The junta lamented his death but refused to authorize a state funeral. —Ed.]

Although many, if not most of its future goals were unclear, the junta made unmistakable its determination to change the leftward course of Allende's foreign policy. One of its first acts was to break relations with Cuba, which Allende had recognized soon after his inauguration, in defiance of the Organization of American States ban. A few hours after Allende died, 150 Cubans were hustled to Santiago's . . . airport and put aboard a plane for home. . . .

Castro, who had been an enthusiastic ally of Allende, charged that "US imperialism had put down the revolutionary movement." Political leaders all across Latin America voiced their revulsion at the death of democracy in Chile. Mexican President Luis Echeverría, who had provided both financial and moral support for the Allende government, recalled his ambassador and offered asylum to any Chilean who sought it, specifically to Mrs. Allende. She refused at first, but at week's end changed her mind and accepted the offer. The Mexican government also ordered three days of official mourning, the first time it had so honored a foreign head of government since the assassination of John F. Kennedy.

Elsewhere in the world, there were clear signs that the Chilean president had gained instant martyrdom among radicals, alongside Patrice Lumumba of the Congo (now Zaïre) and [the Latin American] Che Guevara. In Paris, a crowd of thirty thousand marched through the streets shouting, "Down with the murderers and the CIA!" In Rome, there were sympathetic work stoppages and eulogies proclaiming that "Allende is an idea that does not die." Even moderate politicians publicly regretted that another republic had succumbed to rule by junta. The West German government, for instance, expressed its "deep dismay" and its hope that "democratic conditions will soon return to Chile."

One country was conspicuously silent: the US. The Nixon Administration had been antagonistic to Allende ever since he emerged as the likely winner of the 1970 presidential campaign. Washington's hostility increased after Allende's new government fully nationalized copper mines and other industrial properties owned by US companies and declined to pay several of them compensation. Relations between the two countries grew worse when it was revealed that multinational ITT had offered the United States Government more than $1 million to help prevent Allende's election, and had held discussions with the CIA on possible ways to keep him out of office.

The Nixon Administration did what it could to make life for Allende uncomfortable, mostly through financial pressure on institutions like the World Bank. In August 1971, as a result of US complaints that debt-laden Chile was a poor credit risk, the Export-Import Bank refused to make a $21 million loan to Lan-Chile airline to enable it to buy three Boeing jets, even though the airline had a perfect repayment record. US exports to Chile overall declined 50 percent during Allende's three years.

Military Rapport

But the Pentagon remained on relatively good terms with Chile's military brass. . . . [In 1972] for instance, the US extended $10 million to the Chilean air force to buy transport planes and other equipment. The military rapport was so solid, in fact, that stories were circulating in Washington . . . that US officials had known about the coup up to sixteen hours before it took place.

White House spokesmen denied that the Administration had had any such foreknowledge. There had been many rumors—with many different dates—of a possible coup, they insisted, but nothing solid had been known until La Moneda was actually stormed. In any case, the US had not moved to alert Allende on the ground that to do so would have been interfering in the internal affairs of another nation. The explanation was obviously not strong enough to dispel the suspicion that the US had played some part in engineering the Chilean president's overthrow.

Allende bore much of the blame for his own downfall. His socialist fiscal policies shattered Chile's economy instead of helping it. Always a net importer of food, the country had to import still more because Allende's land-reform programs reduced production. The government, as owner of the copper mines, was in deep trouble when world copper prices fell. Foreign reserves totaled $345 million when Allende took office; by the end of . . . [1972] they had disappeared, and Chile was forced to plead for rescheduling of more than $2.5 billion in international debts. The country was so polarized in the end that Allende was under simultaneous attack by rightists for being too extreme and by leftists for being too timid.

Few Chileans were neutral about the president. Although their lavish lifestyle was only marginally diminished, the rich—5 percent of the population controlling 20 percent of its resources—despised him for seizing the property from which their wealth had come. The middle class, squeezed by inflation and plagued with shortages, was bitter and unreconcilable. Hundreds, perhaps thousands of Chileans left the country. Others who remained kept one-way airline tickets at hand just in case.

Still, Allende had plenty of admirers. Some were not even socialists, but sympathetic liberals who hoped that he could succeed in bridging the gulf between the poor and the wealthy. The poor, peasant and worker alike, idolized him. "I would be a hypocrite if I were to say that I am president of all Chileans," he once observed. . . .

Allende slept only five hours a night and spent most of his waking hours working. "To work for the people is really a pleasure," he once said grandiosely. Allende impressed visitors as a crisp administrator. He was a hard man but not a ruthless one. . . .

Despite his Marxist beliefs, Allende savored the good life. He drank Scotch, liked golf and was fond of good wines. In addition to his family home, he reportedly had a hideaway to which he would take cronies—and women—and barbecue steaks for them. Allende was a sophisticated but casual dresser who favored turtleneck sweaters even at work. In fact, he was reportedly wearing a white turtleneck when he died. After the fighting died down last week, the military government televised a film showing Allende's imposing wardrobe and shelves of imported liquor and foods. The implication was hard to miss: while his supporters had been queuing up, Allende had engaged in the kind of hoarding he railed against.

Allende's family dated back to the early days of Chile. His physician grandfather was a Masonic grandmaster and the founder of the first nonreligious elementary school in predominantly Roman Catholic Chile. Allende's father was a notary who died while his son was serving one of many prison terms for socialist activity. Allende was allowed to attend the funeral. At the graveside he delivered an impromptu speech pledging himself to seek freedom for the people and social justice. He became a doctor but gave up medicine for politics. He campaigned doggedly until, on the fourth attempt, he was finally elected president.

Once in office, Allende moved swiftly to change the economic face of the country. His Christian Democratic predecessor, Eduardo Frei, had already introduced agrarian reforms and pushed government participation in industry. But Allende inaugurated a far more sweeping program of government ownership and operation, beginning with total ownership of the giant copper operations, whose US owners had been woefully slow in training Chileans for more important, better paying jobs. Cement, steel, electricity and telephones were also nationalized, along with both foreign and domestic banks. Labor unions were given control of new plants that went up in belts around Santiago, close by tidy neighbors of the middle class. With the government's tacit consent, peasants seized huge estates owned by absentee landlords, and in their zeal even took land from small farmers.

In office Allende made at least two crucial political mistakes. One was to forget—or at least ignore—the fact that he had entered office as a minority winner. In the tumultuous 1970 election, Allende led the two other candidates, but gained only 36.3 percent of the popular vote. According to the constitution, the Chilean congress was called on to choose the winner. It followed tradition by selecting Allende, the front runner. He thus became president even though nearly two thirds of the voters preferred other men. But he ruled as though he had the nation behind him.

March of the Pots

Allende's second mistake was to assume that the middle and upper classes would placidly accept his "Chilean road to socialism" so long as all things were done constitutionally. They never did. "If we have to burn half of Chile to save it from communism, then we will do it," threatened . . . [the] leader of an extremist right-wing organization called Fatherland and Liberty. More moderate opponents were less outraged but equally adamant against Allende's plans to broaden state controls. Opposition parties, controlling both houses of congress, fought him all the time he was in power.

Some of the strongest opposition came from Chilean women, perhaps the most liberated in Latin America. As occasional meatless days became regular meatless weeks, they organized a "March of the Empty Pots" in 1971 to dramatize the rising cost and increasing shortage of food. The sound of spoons banging against empty pots became a symbolic klaxon of protest. The signal would suddenly begin in one quarter of Santiago and ripple all across the city, to the chagrin of the government. . . . After Allende's supporters staged a massive rally in Plaza de la Constitución to celebrate the third anniversary of his election, 100,000 women turned out a day later for a counterdemonstration. They were dispersed with tear gas.

The principal cause of Allende's downfall was his inability to settle a series of crippling strikes—staged not by leftist labor unions but by the president's implacable middle-class enemies. . . . Workers at El Teniente, the world's largest underground copper mine, marched out on a seventy-four-day strike for higher wages that cost the government nearly $75 million in lost revenue.

The unrest spread. Three weeks after the copper strike was settled, the powerful truckers (most of the country's commerce travels by road) went out on strike again. They had first struck in . . . [1972], complaining about a lack of spare parts and the government's increasing trucking operations. This time they charged that Allende had reneged on agreements . . . to ease both situations. The new strike cost Chile nearly $6 million a day as food supplies dwindled, fuel vanished and crop shortages loomed because seeds and fertilizer could not be delivered. . . .

Meanwhile, the political polarization of Chile continued, with Allende seemingly unable to do much about it. The truckers' protest triggered sporadic strikes by doctors, shopkeepers and bus and taxi drivers angered by ballooning inflation . . . and meager incomes. To prevent chaos, the president tried to make peace with the opposition Christian Democrats. Nothing came of the dialogue because the party was badly split. One faction urged support for the government. Another, led by ex-President Frei, was determined to help topple it by withholding cooperation.

In an effort to reduce right-wing opposition and frighten the truckers, Allende persuaded commanders of the armed forces to come into his cabinet. That was a serious error, since it politicized the military, which had tried to stay above the crisis, into pro- and anti-Allende factions. The result was a charade of revolving-door politics.

Less than ten days after he had been appointed public works minister with responsibility for settling the truckers' strike, air force General César Ruiz Danyau resigned, charging that he had not been given enough authority. Anti-Allende factions within the military then forced General Carlos Prats González, the army's commander in chief, to resign as minister of defense. He was replaced by General Pinochet, now president of the junta.

The reunited Christian Democrats greeted the coup with jubilation. They issued a junta-approved statement deploring the violence but offering support for Chile's new leaders. The party statement went on to note that the Christian Democrats were certain that power would be returned "to the sovereign people" as soon as "the burdensome tasks of the junta have been completed."

Tragic History

Later . . . the new interior minister, General Bonilla, promised that Chile would be returned to civilian rule, but did not say when. Most observers assumed that the military would be in power quite some time—long enough, at any rate, to try to wipe out whatever vestiges of Marxism remain in the country.

Democracy has all too often been the victim of South America's tragic history of violence and upheaval. Today fully 70 percent of its . . . [220] million people are subject to some kind of military rule. In many cases the officers ousted leftist or populist leaders, such as Brazil's João Goulart or Guatemala's Jacobo Arbenz, who had tried to change their nation's rigidly oligarchic structures. Allende is the latest in this line of ambitious but unsuccessful reformers.

Chile's military junta succeeded in its basic goal, getting rid of Allende, but the real question is: At what cost? As a spiritual inspiration to leftists, Allende may prove to be more potent dead than alive. On the other hand, his overthrow may convince radicals that a violent revolution, repressing all dissent, is the only sure way to socialism. Certainly this "decent, godless man" will never be forgotten by the poor of Chile, who regarded him as a secular savior. Which means that the next time a popular Marxist leader appears in Chile, his path to power may not be quite so peaceful.

REPRESSION IN CHILE [3]

There is little doubt that most Chileans welcomed the armed forces' overthrow of the Marxist government of Presi-

[3] From "Continuing Repression Repels Many in Chile Who Backed Coup," by Everett G. Martin, staff reporter. *Wall Street Journal.* p 1+. My. 13, '74. Reprinted with permission of *The Wall Street Journal* © 1974 Dow Jones & Company, Inc. All rights reserved.

dent Salvador Allende last September [1973]. But now, after more than half a year of stern rule by a four-man military junta—and with no end in sight—many aren't sure they like what's going on.

They are especially worried by the junta's continued use of repressive tactics to head off any threat, whether real or imagined, against law and order. Almost anyone can be denounced anonymously and disappear without his relatives having any idea where he has been taken. There have been cases of torture. Estimates of the number of political prisoners being held without charges range as high as 6,000.

Besides the arrests, some 38,000 workers are reported to have been fired from their jobs in government and industry, on the ground that they were active supporters of Dr. Allende. A low-ranking labor leader, who opposed the Marxists, argues that the time has come to forgive these people.

Those who were fired can't find jobs [he says]. They are being demolished. It was, after all, legitimate to support the former government, but now they are being persecuted and hunted for it. It isn't fair. They acted in good faith.

A Number of Pluses

Still, Chileans like many aspects of the regime. They welcome the public calm enforced by the strict military discipline after three years of escalating violence under the Marxists. They also welcome these developments:

Government services are functioning again; most factories are operating normally; severe shortages of basic necessities have ended; the black market has dried up; public-housing construction is going ahead again; schoolchildren are getting free breakfasts and lunches as part of a drive to improve nutrition for the poor.

Chileans don't like the inflation—prices went up 57 percent in the first quarter [of 1974]—but it is recognized that the inflation was inherited from Dr. Allende, and people don't expect the junta to end it overnight. At least it's being slowed down.

Opinions are mixed about the junta's having put all political parties, even those opposed to the Marxists, in indefinite limbo, a measure designed to end Chile's traditionally heated political wrangling over every issue. Wives of copper miners cheered army General Augusto Pinochet, junta president, when he told them to "erase from your minds the idea of elections."

The Main Concern

But it is the repression that most disturbs Chileans at all levels. Where genuine Marxist extremists are concerned, the junta probably does have a security problem. During the Allende regime, a quantity of weapons was apparently smuggled into the country to arm leftist extremists. Almost weekly, intelligence agents report uncovering another small cache of them. Moreover, pro-Allende Chileans who fled the country after the coup are openly soliciting funds to finance a guerrilla campaign in Chile.

Recently a series of forest fires—started, according to the authorities, with gasoline—threatened the port city of Valparaíso. A small bomb was exploded on the docks there, and there have been numerous other suspicious fires in the city.

One youthful extremist, who is still in hiding, told a relative he secretly visited that his organization was planning political kidnappings like those committed by Argentine terrorists. Such talk may be futile blustering, but the junta does worry about national security. Any kind of terrorist outbreak would, for one thing, hurt the junta's efforts to attract foreign investors to spur Chile's economic growth. In a recent speech, General Pinochet declared:

If the submerged elements try to rise against our people, we will not hesitate to react with drastic means. Until we have caught them all, I will not lift the military measures.

An Array of Zealots

A bewildering array of six different intelligence groups is busy chasing down suspected terrorists with frightening zeal. There is an intelligence service in each of the three branches of the armed forces, one in the police, a joint organization and, finally, a new superagency.

One man, a political commentator during the Allende years, was seized by army intelligence, was interrogated for days and then was sent home with written instructions to consider himself under house arrest and responsible to the army. Soon afterward, members of the air force broke in on him. Ignoring his army documents, they held him for several days trying to torture information out of him. When they released him, by then a broken man, he took asylum in a foreign embassy.

Most cases of brutality and torture seem to lead back to the air force, although no one knows if the perpetrators are acting as members of air force intelligence or as members of the new superagency. There have been cases of army commanders intervening to get detainees out of the hands of air force agents—an indication that the armed forces themselves may be divided over the use of such extreme methods.

The number of political prisoners being held without charges fluctuates, of course, as some are released and others picked up. A group of Santiago lawyers who protested the situation in a private letter to the junta were soundly denounced as being "unpatriotic," but such protest may have had an impact: Since then, a group of air force officers charged with having been pro-Allende and anti–air force before the coup have been represented by outspoken defense lawyers during their trial, and the trial was open to invited foreign observers; likewise, imprisoned former officials of the Allende government have been scheduled for early public trials, also with defense lawyers representing them and with invited foreign observers on hand.

Although most detainees are eventually released, one college professor expresses a widespread sentiment when he says, "We don't like this feeling of being unprotected against arrests. Lots of mistakes are being made."

While the rate of arrests has slowed down measurably

since the first weeks after the coup, the junta has developed a new concern that, to many Chileans, borders on paranoia. The military leaders now appear to be zeroing in on a new class of so-called enemies that seems to include anyone who is critical of them.

The rector of a university in Valparaíso was sacked recently for being "antijunta." The head of the Catholic University television station and several members of his staff, all of whom were leaders in the fight against the Marxists, were also fired, and it is presumed that they, too, had "antijunta" tendencies. Meanwhile, General Pinochet has issued a dark warning that many civil servants are also going to go.

These people pretend to be cooperating [he said], but according to information that we have, in reality they are not cooperating. They always say yes to you, but when the moment comes to act they move slowly, they mislay documents, they change a word or a comma. They may comply with an order, but privately they talk against it.

It isn't entirely a coincidence that most of "these people" happen to be Christian Democrats. Relations between the military and the Christian Democrats have never been good. When the Christian Democrats were in power during the administration of President Eduardo Frei, just before the Allende government, they ignored the military men or treated them with disdain until one army unit staged a revolt in its barracks to demand higher pay. As one party member explains it, "The Christian Democrats regard the military as a bunch of fools, and the military regard the politicians as a bunch of crooks."

They Mean to Stay

Except for its left wing, however, the party supported the coup as the only way to stop the Marxists. Observers point out, though, that many of the party leaders expected the military to turn the government over to them after a short caretaker period.

Now the military has made it clear that it intends to stay and make sweeping changes.

Some politicians [General Pinochet said in a major speech . . . in April 1974] initially took a favorable attitude toward the government, but they thought when the armed forces took action to liberate Chile that the conduct of the state would be returned to them in a short time. Today they react antagonistically because they realize that they were wrong, and I ask myself, "Are they patriots or mercenaries?"

The politicians, he implies, are responsible for demagoguery.

It is necessary to eliminate demagoguery, the principal sickness of Chile [he says]. From it has come the sectarianism which divides and the inefficiency which impedes progress and justice. This sickness is not only from the past three years. It is much older than that.

General Pinochet's barely disguised attacks on the Christian Democrats go down well with many conservative Chileans who blame the liberal Frei government for opening the door for the Marxists with its land-reform program and other measures.

Christian Democrats, whose adherents make up a substantial portion of the middle class, rankle at having no voice in governmental affairs and at the pointed criticism they are taking. They retort with some sharp barbs of their own.

The junta should recognize [says one party member] that the political parties fought the Marxists for three years while the military were the right hand of Allende. They were in opposition one day. They shouldn't look down on people who were fighting for three years.

One of the most outspoken critics of the Christian Democrats is the government's chief press spokesman, Alvaro Puga. To a request for an explanation of the junta's opinion of the party, he replies:

Before Allende the Christian Democrats paved the road for the Marxists because they began to talk in the style of Henry Kissinger—of a dialogue with the Marxists. They talked of communitarianism instead of communism, but people without perception believed that they were both equal within democracy. . . . During Allende, they were a moderating element between the Marxists who wanted dictatorship and the rightists who wanted to overthrow the Marxists. They were the silver bridge—beautiful but weak—between the Marxists and the Democrats.

. . . Mr. Puga came to prominence during the Allende regime, delivering biting criticism of the Marxists over the radio and in a newspaper column written under the pen name "Alexis." No one can quite explain how he rose to such an influential position in the junta, but he is one of a group of puritanical young Roman Catholic ultraconservatives who seem to play a significant role in outlining the public philosophy of the junta. This group is known for its dislike of the Christian Democrats.

Mr. Puga's statements cause dismay in other branches of the government. A foreign ministry official, for example, winced when he heard of Mr. Puga's reference to Mr. Kissinger. "How can he say such things?" the official said. "We are rather pleased with Mr. Kissinger."

Mr. Puga outlines a form of government for Chile where the only elections would be in neighborhood organizations and professional and labor groups. These grass-roots organizations would transmit their needs to the local mayor, who would tell the governor, who would get in touch with the junta. There doesn't seem to be any room in the system for national political parties, and Mr. Puga says: "We want to make a mechanism where it is not necessary to have political parties to have a position on a question."

It was Mr. Puga who ordered the Christian Democrats' radio network closed for six days because of broadcasts commenting unfavorably on the state of human rights in Chile. Soon thereafter, the archbishops of Chile issued a call for reconciliation. It said:

For love of our fatherland, we must contribute to reestablish-
ing a harmonious atmosphere in which all Chileans can live and
be brothers. . . . The basic condition for living together peacefully
is the establishment of a state of law in which the constitution
and the law will be a guarantee for everyone."

BIBLIOGRAPHY

An asterisk (*) preceding a reference indicates that the article or a part of it has been reprinted in this book.

BOOKS, PAMPHLETS, AND DOCUMENTS

Alba, Victor. Alliance without allies: the mythology of progress in Latin America. Praeger. '65.

Alexander, R. J. An introduction to Argentina. Praeger. '69.

Alisky, M. H. Uruguay: a contemporary survey. Praeger. '69.

Bailey, N. A. Latin America in world politics. Walker. '67.

Bemis, S. F. The Latin American policy of the United States: an historical interpretation. Norton. '67.

*Bradford, C. I. Jr. Forces for change in Latin America: U.S. policy implications. Overseas Development Council. 1717 Massachusetts Ave. N.W. Washington, D.C. 20036. '71.

Cornelius, W. A. and Fagen, R. R. eds. Political power in Latin America: seven confrontations. Prentice-Hall. '70.

Debray, Régis. The Chilean revolution: conversations with Allende. Pantheon. '72.
Translation of *La vie cilena,* originally published 1971 in Milan, Italy.

Delpar, Helen, ed. Encyclopedia of Latin America. McGraw-Hill. '74.

*Foreign Policy Association. Great decisions (1975). The Association. 345 E. 46th St. New York 10017. '75.
Reprinted in this book: Excerpts from Fact Sheet no 3. Brazil: pacesetter for Latin America. p 33-6.

Gilbert, Alan. Latin American development: a geographical perspective. Penguin. '75.

Gott, Richard. Guerrilla movements in Latin America. Doubleday. '71.

Goulet, Denis. The cruel choice: a new concept in the theory of development. Atheneum. '71.

Gray, R. B. ed. Latin America and the United States in the 1970's. Peacock. '71.

Hanke, L. U. Contemporary Latin America: a short history. Van Nostrand. '68.

Herring, H. C. A history of Latin America from the beginnings to the present. Knopf. '55.

Hilton, Ronald, ed. The movement toward Latin American unity. Praeger. '69.

Humphreys, R. A. ed. Tradition and revolt in Latin America, and other essays. Columbia University Press. '69.

Inter-American Development Bank. Development trends. The Bank. 808 17th St. N.W. Washington, D.C. 20577. '74.

*International Bank for Reconstruction and Development. The World Bank Group in the Americas. The Bank. 1818 H St. N.W. Washington, D.C. 20433. '74.

James, P. E. Latin America. Odyssey. '69.

Lazar, Arpad von. Latin American politics: a primer. Allyn and Bacon. '71.

Levinson, Jerome and De Onís, Juan. The alliance that lost its way: a critical report on the Alliance for Progress. Quadrangle. '70.

McClellan, G. S. ed. U.S. policy in Latin America. (Reference Shelf, v 35 no 1) Wilson. '63.

Malloy, J. M. Bolivia: the uncompleted revolution. University of Pittsburgh Press. '70.

Martz, J. D. ed. The dynamics of change in Latin American politics. Prentice-Hall. '71.

Mercier Vega, Luis. Guerrillas in Latin America: the technique of counterstate. Praeger. '69.

Nelson, Michael. The development of tropical lands: policy issues in Latin America. Johns Hopkins University Press (for Resources for the Future). '73.

Organization of American States. General Secretariat. Latin America's development and the Alliance for Progress. The Organization. Washington, D.C. 20006. '73.

Perloff, H. S. Alliance for Progress: a social invention in the making. Johns Hopkins Press (for Resources for the Future). '69.

Plaza, Galo. Latin America: today and tomorrow. Acropolis. '71.
Excerpts. Américas. 23:41-3. Je. '71.

Poppino, R. E. Brazil: the land and people. 2d ed. Oxford University Press. '73.

Prebisch, Raúl. Change and development: Latin America's great task; report submitted to the Inter-American Development Bank. Praeger. '70.

Reed, I. B. The Latin American scene of the seventies. University of Miami. Center for Advanced International Studies. Suite 1213. 1730 Rhode Island Ave. N.W. Washington, D.C. 20036. '72.

Rockefeller, N. A. The Rockefeller report on the Americas; the official report of a U.S. presidential mission for the Western Hemisphere. Quadrangle. '69.

Rosenbaum, H. J. and Tyler, W. G. Contemporary Brazil: issues in economic and political development. Praeger. '72.

Sauvage, Léo. Che Guevara: the failure of a revolutionary. Prentice-Hall. '73.

*Schneider, R. M. Latin American panorama. (Headline Series no 178) Foreign Policy Association. 345 E. 46th St. New York 10017. '66.

Sigmund, P. E. ed. Models of political change in Latin America. Praeger. '70.

Stepan, Alfred. The military in politics: changing patterns in Brazil. Princeton University Press. '71.

*Stephansky, B. S. Latin America: toward a new nationalism. (Headline Series no 211) Foreign Policy Association. 345 E. 46th St. New York 10017. '72.

Szulc, Tad. Latin America. Atheneum. '66.

Szulc, Tad. The winds of revolution: Latin America today and tomorrow. Praeger. '63.

Von Lazar, Aroad. Latin American politics: a primer. Allyn and Bacon. '71.

Wagley, Charles. An introduction to Brazil. Columbia University Press. '71.

Walsh, W. B. Yanqui, come back! the story of Hope in Peru. Dutton. '66.

Williams, Byron. Continent in turmoil. Parents' Magazine Press. '71.

Worcester, D. E. Brazil: from colony to world power. Scribner. '73.

PERIODICALS

America. 120:266-7. Mr. 8, '69. Anti-capitalism in Latin America.

America. 122:160-1. F. 14, '70. Target in Peru: social transformation. P. L. Ruggere.

America. 122:646-9. Je. 20, '70. Brazil's revolution six years later. A. A. Lima.

America. 124:203-7. F. 27, '71. Family planning in Latin America: image and reality. T. G. Sanders.

America. 125:67-9. Ag. 7, 71. Colonialism lives in South America. E. K. Culhane.

America. 128:308-9. Ap. 7, '73. Brazil: how far toward democracy? Agostino Bono.

America. 129:436. D. 8, '73. Human rights in Chile.

America. 130:151-2. Mr. 2, '74. Old problems for Brazil's new president. D. L. Kirchner.

America. 130:490-3. Je. 22, '74. Tree grows in Peru. A. J. Ledesma.

Américas. 21:44. My. '69. Development progress in Latin America.

Américas. 23:37-40. Mr. '71. Economics and development of modern Brazil. F. J. Munch.

Américas. 25:44-5. O. '73. Hemisphere: economic development.

Américas. 26:19-49. Mr. '74. Past twenty-five years; chronological narrative of events.

Business Week. p 56-7+. My. 17, '69. Argentina steps up its tempo.

Business Week. p 34-5. N. 14, '70. Highway to save the stricken northeast: trans-Amazon highway.

Business Week. p 90-3. Mr. 13, '71. Booming Brazil finds a key to growth; with editorial comment.
   Editorial comment. Business Week. p 136. Mr. 13, '71.

Business Week. p 31. S. 4, '71. Investors shy from a shaky economy.

Business Week. p 38. Jl. 21, '73. Argentina: foreign business pins hope on Perón.

Business Week. p 44+. Ag. 12, '73. Chile: economic chaos in Allende country.

Business Week. p 30-1. S. 29, '73. Future for business in Chile.

Business Week. p 41-2+. N. 17, '73. Chile: an uphill struggle to revive business.

Business Week. p 51. D. 8, '73. Venezuela: nationalizing oil is a presidential priority.

Business Week. p 32. Ja. 12, '74. Brazil: striving to become an export superpower.

Business Week. p 34. Jl. 13, '74. Argentina: Perón's social pact begins to crack.

Business Week. p 30-1. Ag. 3, '74. Chile: a wobbly economy needs foreign help.

Business Week. p 34+. Ag. 31, '74. Venezuela: edging toward nationalization.

Christian Century. 87:1163-4. S. 30, '70. Political avalanche occurs in Chile. J. S. Bradshaw.

Christian Century. 90:1044-5. O. 24, '73. What happened in Chile? E. J. Holland.

Christian Century. 91:404-5. Ap. 10, '74. Argentina's year under Perón. Argenticus (pseudonym).

Christian Century. 91:546-8. My. 15, '74. Bolivia: turbulent tides and an oppressive aftermath. Justo Latino.

Christian Science Monitor. p 1+. Ja. 8, '73. Guerrillas fare poorly in Latin America. J. N. Goodsell.

Christian Science Monitor. p 3A. Je. 27, '74. Latin Americans all too familiar with double-digit inflation.

Christian Science Monitor. p 3A. Jl. 15, '74. Stroessner serving fifth term as Paraguay's president.

Commonweal. 94:331-6. Je. 25, '71. Latin America: who is to blame? Gary Maceoin.

Commonweal. 95:244-5. D. 10, '71. Chile con Allende. D. D. Ranstead.
   Editorial comment. Commonweal. 95:253-6. D. 10, '71.

Commonweal. 97:268-9. D. 22, '72. Repression in Bolivia. Roberto Valda.

Commonweal. 99:103-5. N. 2, '73. Chilean coup; an eyewitness report.

Commonweal. 99:356-8. Ja. 11, '74. Ecuador: up from bananas; growing nationalism in Venezuela, Peru and Ecuador. Agostino Bono.

Commonweal. 99:476-7. F. 15, '74. Peru: creeping at a petty pace. Agostino Bono.

Commonweal. 100:522-3. S. 27, '74. Ms. Peron. Agostino Bono.

Current History. 56:352-4+. Je. '69. Latin American military elite. T. M. Millington.

Current History. 58:65-117. F. '70. Latin America: symposium.

Current History. 60:65-111+. F. '71. Latin America, 1971; symposium.

*Current History. 62:65-108+. F. '72. Latin America, 1972; symposium.

Reprinted in this book: Uruguay's lost paradise. p 98-103.

*Current History. 64:19-80+. F. '73. Latin America, 1973; symposium.

Reprinted in this book: Problems in Allende's Chile. Alan Angell. p 57-60+.

Current History. 66:1-30+. Ja. '74. Latin America, 1974; symposium.

Department of State Bulletin. 62:179-85. F. 16, '70. Trade, capital, and Latin American development; address, January 19, 1970. N. Samuels.

Department of State Bulletin. 65:236-8. Ag. 30, '71. Sustaining a meaningful commitment to Latin American development; statement, August 4, 1971. C. A. Meyer.

Department of State Bulletin. 68:937-41. Je. 25, '73. United States–Latin American economic relations; address, May 21, 1973. W. J. Casey.

Economist. 248:16+. S. 15, '73. End of Allende.

Economist. 248:50. S. 15, '73. Modest millionaire [Perón].

Economist. 249:43-4+. O. 13, '73. Chile after Allende.

Focus. 18:1-6. D. '67. Paraguay. R. E. Crist.

Focus. 23:1-8. F. '73. Unemployment: bitter burden of millions in South America; adaptation of address, May 17, 1971. D. A. Morse.

Focus. 24:1-8. O. '73. Bolivia. R. J. Tata.

Focus. 24:1-8. D. '73. Argentina. M. D. Winsberg.

Foreign Affairs. 48:494-508. Ap. '70. Alliance rhetoric versus Latin American reality. A. F. Lowenthal.

Foreign Affairs. 49:442-53. Ap. '71. Chilean experiment. Claudio Véliz.

Foreign Affairs. 49:454-63. Ap. '71. Revolutionary nationalism in Peru. Marcel Niedergang.

Foreign Affairs. 49:464-79. Ap. '71. Brazil: all power to the generals. H. J. Stein and D. M. Trubek.

Foreign Affairs. 50:83-96. O. '71. Second Latin American revolution. Eduardo Frei Montalva.

Foreign Affairs. 52:322-40. Ja. '74. Invisible blockade and the overthrow of Allende. P. E. Sigmund.

*Foreign Affairs. 52:799-817. Jl. '74. Peru's ambiguous revolution. A. F. Lowenthal.

*Fortune. 90:138-43+. Ag. '74. Suddenly it's mañana in Latin America. Richard Armstrong.

*Nation. 215:17-20. Jl. 10, '72. Brazil: the imitative society. E. B. Burns.

National Review. 23:860-3. Ag. 10, '71. Don't underestimate Brazil. Selden Rodman.

National Review. 23:1348-50+. D. 3, '71. What drives Latin Americans left? Selden Rodman.

National Review. 24:517-19+. My. 12, '72. After the prosperity, the problems. Selden Rodman.

National Review. 26:1043+. S. 13, '74. Letter from Argentina. Nena Ossa.

Nation's Business. 60:62-3. My. '72. Toward a brighter mañana. G. E. Bradley.

New Politics. 10:56-70. Winter '73. Latin America's trend to the right. Sidney Lens.

New Republic. 163:8-9. N. 28, '70. Expectations in Chile. W. R. Long.

New Republic. 164:20-1. Ja. 2, '71. Progress is not just around the corner. D. F. Ross.

New Republic. 168:5-6. Ap. 14, '73. Brute force of money; ITT's attempt to intervene in Chilean politics.

New Republic. 168:21-3. Je. 30, '73. US and ITT in Chile. Tad Szulc.

New Republic. 171:13-15. S. 28. '74. Where President Ford is wrong: candid but mistaken about Chile. Tad Szulc.

New York Times. p 1+. O. 6, '73. Kissinger calls on Latins to join in "new dialogue." Bernard Gwertzman.

*New York Times. p 2. Ja. 3, '74. Venezuela grows fast, but many stay poor. Marvine Howe.

New York Times. p 18. F. 10, '74. Bolivia's burden: widespread want.

New York Times. p 2. Mr. 13, '74. Uruguay, in decline, awaits full military take-over. Jonathan Kandell.

New York Times. p 2. Mr. 15, '74. Caracas poor look to new president. Marvine Howe.

New York Times. p 7. Mr. 27, '74. Student unrest mounts in Brazil. Marvine Howe.

New York Times. p 7. Mr. 28, '74. Junta's grip felt in Chilean slums. Jonathan Kandell.

New York Times. p E 5. Ap. 7, '74. In Brazil, all is not as it seems. Marvine Howe.

New York Times. p E 5. Ap. 7, '74. Perón's return to Argentina has failed to bring unity. Jonathan Kandell.

New York Times. p F 1+. Ap. 14, '74. Test for Brazil's inflation. Marvine Howe.

New York Times. p 37. Jl. 9, '74. Brazil: cost of growth. Graham Hovey.

New York Times. p 1+. S. 13, '74. Chile's junta after a year. Jonathan Kandell.

New York Times. p E 5. S. 15, '74. The junta has turned Chile into a police state. Jonathan Kandell.

New York Times. p 2. N. 9, '74. In Quito now, even day of dead is lively. Jonathan Kandell.

*New York Times. p 2. Ja. 21, '75. Stroessner gives "peace" to Paraguay, but at a price. Jonathan Kandell.

New York Times. p 2. Ja. 23, '75. On Argentina's fertile pampas, the bitter harvest of neglect. Jonathan Kandell.

New York Times. p 3. Ja. 24, '75. 20 Latin countries condemn U.S. trade act. David Binder.

New York Times. p 8. Ja. 28, '75. Latins, upset over trade, postpone talks with U.S.

New York Times. p 1+. F. 6, '75. Peruvian troops crush police revolt in capital. Jonathan Kandell.

New York Times. p 2. Mr. 10, '75. Chile's agriculture makes a fast comeback. Jonathan Kandell.

New York Times. p 10. Mr. 20, '75. Beleaguered Mrs. Peron clings to power, but Argentines ask, How long? Jonathan Kandell.

New York Times Magazine. p 52-3+. D. 7, '69. Report from Brazil: what the Left is saying. José Yglesias.

New York Times Magazine. p 26-7+. N. 1, '70. Chileans have elected a revolution. Norman Gall.

New York Times Magazine. p 16-17+. D. 17, '72. Opposition in Chile. Juan De Onís.

New Yorker. 45:32-4. S. 6, '69. Paraguay. Donald Barthelme.

New Yorker. 46:80-9. Ja. 30, '71. Letter from Santiago. Joseph Kraft.

New Yorker. 50:100+. S. 16, '74. Letter from Guyana. Jane Kramer.

New Yorker. 50:278. S. 30, '74. Notes and comment; CIA intervention in Chile.

Newsweek. 77:60+. Ap. 19, '71. Chile: it's half and half.

Newsweek. 80:39-40. N. 27, '72. Argentina: the return of El Viejo.

Newsweek. 81:83+. Mr. 12, '73. How Brazil flies with inflation.

Newsweek. 82:29-30. Jl. 23, '73. Perón's stage-managed comeback.

Newsweek. 82:42-3+. S. 24, '73. Chile: the brutal death of an idea.

Newsweek. 82:42-4+. O. 1, '73. Chile: the junta's iron rule.

Newsweek. 82:50+. O. 15, '73. Exiles; pro-Allende foreign exiles.

*Newsweek. 84:35-7. Jl. 15, '74. Argentina after Perón; a man on horseback.

Newsweek. 84:41. S. 9, '74. La presidente: Isabel Perón.

Newsweek. 84:51-2. S. 23, '74. CIA's new Bay of Bucks.

Political Science Quarterly. 87:401-18. S. '72. Soldiers in politics: new insights on Latin American armed forces. E. H. Hyman.

Progressive. 38:35-40. F. '74. Chile: the dream bides time. Pat Garrett and Adam Schesch.

Progressive. 38:31-4. Je. '74. Democracy, Colombian style. Alan Riding.

Ramparts. 12:25-30. Je. '74. Chile: can the junta rule? Richard Pierson.

Reader's Digest. 100:118-21. F. '72. Two faces of Brazil: boom extraordinary. Scott Seegers and K. W. Seegers.

Reader's Digest. 100:121-4. F. '72. Two faces of Brazil: withered freedom. Trevor Armbrister.

Saturday Review. 52:10-13. Ag. 16, '69. Tinderbox in Latin America. S. M. Linowitz.

Saturday Review. 55:64-5. Jl. 1, '72. Guyana: three points of Eden. Jan Carew.

Saturday Review/World. 1:12-15. O. 23, '73. Military rule; can it spark a new Latin self-reliance? Max Lerner.

Saturday Review/World. 1:42-3+. O. 23, '73. Brazil puts a boom in the bossa nova. Joseph Sims.

*Saturday Review/World. 1:12-13+. Ap. 20, '74. Kissinger's "new dialogue." Alan Riding.

Saturday Review/World. 1:16+. Ap. 20, '74. The perennial Perón. Henry Raymont.

Saturday Review/World. 1:37-9. Je. 29, '74. After the coup: a Latin American how-to. Fay Haussman.

School & Society. 99:361-4. O. '71. Education, revolution and nationalism in Peru. R. G. Paulston.

School & Society. 99:439-42. N. '71. Education, population, and the quality of life in Latin America. Kenneth Holland.

Senior Scholastic. 102:4-5. Mr. 19, '73. Argentina in anguish.

Senior Scholastic. 102:8-9. Mr. 19, '73. Left face in Chile.

Time. 97:33+. F. 22, '71. Allende's hundred days.

Time. 98:32-3. Jl. 26, '71. Bolivia: man in the middle.

Time. 100:29-30+. N. 27, '72. Dictator returns to his past; Peronism: our sun, our air, our water.

Time. 102:23-4. Jl. 2, '73. Second coming of Perón.

Time. 102:25-6. Jl. 9, '73. Chile: right-wing revolt.

Time. 102:25-7. Jl. 9, '73. Trouble, terror and a takeover; Chile, Argentina and Uruguay.

Time. 102:32+. S. 10, '73. Old dictator tries again.

*Time. 102:35-8+. S. 24, '73. Bloody end of a Marxist dream.

Time. 102:26-9. O. 1, '73. Generals consolidate their coup: was the U.S. involved?

Time. 104:72-5B. Jl. 15, '74. Death of *el lider;* Perón: the promise unfulfilled.

Time. 104:21. S. 30, '74. Chile: a case study; CIA intervention.

Time. 104:49. S. 30, '74. The war against Isabel.

Travel. 139:58-63. Je. '73. Colombia, por favor! A. V. Davis.

U.S. News & World Report. 66:36-7. Mr. 10, '69. Nationalist wave hits Latin America; meaning to U.S.

U.S. News & World Report. 66:68-9. Mr. 17, '69. Latin-American showcase where reforms went sour.

U.S. News & World Report. 66:30-2. Je. 16, '69. New turmoil in Latin America; its meaning for U.S.

U.S. News & World Report. 66:50. Je. 23, '69. What Latin Americans want from U.S.

U.S. News & World Report. 67:83-4. D. 22, '69. When inflation gets out of hand: the story of Brazil.

U.S. News & World Report. 68:74-5. Je. 22, '70. How generals are ruling most of a continent.

U.S. News & World Report. 70:39-40. Ap. 19, '71. Can Marxists now go all the way in Chile?

U.S. News & World Report. 71:59-61. Ag. 30, '71. Ailing giant starts a comeback: will it last?

U.S. News & World Report. 71:73-5. O. 25, '71. Road to socialism: a rough one for Chile.

U.S. News & World Report. 73:53-4. Jl. 10, '72. Slowdown on the road to Marxism in Chile.

U.S. News & World Report. 73:47-8+. O. 30, '72. Argentina: deeper in trouble; is Juan Perón the answer?

U.S. News & World Report. 75:44-6. S. 24, '73. New challenge for Chile after a Marxist binge. Joseph Benham.

U.S. News & World Report. 75:59-60. O. 1, '73. Other Latin generals in power: some doing well, some not.

U.S. News & World Report. 75:49-50+. N. 12, '73. Chile takes the cure: belt-tightening, hard work. Joseph Benham.

U.S. News & World Report. 77:60-2. Jl. 22, '74. Next goal is world power, and Brazil is on its way. Joseph Benham.

*U.S. News & World Report. 77:55-6. S. 2, '74. Where chronic inflation brings bewildering results. Joseph Benham.

U.S. News & World Report. 77:33. S. 30, '74. Furor over the CIA—what it's all about.

UNESCO Courier. 25:4-32. Mr. '72. Latin America's cultural explosion; symposium.

*UNICEF News. Issue 80 (1974/2):4-15. '74. Children of the Andes. Alastair Matheson.

*UNICEF News. Issue 80 (1974/2):29-34. '74. Pioneering in Paraguay—a new promise.

Vital Speeches of the Day. 36:418-23. My. 1, '70. Latin America: toward a new policy; address, April 10, 1970. Frank Church.

Wall Street Journal. p 1+. O. 24, '72. Class struggle: the bourgeoisie in Chile battles Allende policy; a civil war is feared. E. G. Martin.

Wall Street Journal. p 6. Jl. 6, '73. The crucial year for Chile's Allende. E. G. Martin.

Wall Street Journal. p 1+. Ap. 19, '74. Allende's legacy: Chile's junta finds it isn't easy getting industry rolling again. E. G. Martin.

*Wall Street Journal. p 1+. My. 13, '74. Second thoughts: continuing repression repels many in Chile who backed coup. E. G. Martin.

Wall Street Journal. p 42. F. 4, '75. Working partners: Peruvian regime seeks labor harmony by giving employes say in management. E. G. Martin.

World Today. 28:483-92. N. '72. Chile's economic reforms: what kind of revolution?

World Today. 29:474-81. N. '73. Brazil's economic miracles. Albert Fishlow.

13-400